JUSTICE

'OUR FATHER IN HEAVEN'

For everyone fighting evil and searching for light.
Never forget the pen is mightier than the sword.

To request permissions, contact the publisher at
publisher@publishedwithlove.biz

FIRST PAPERBACK EDITION 2024
Independently published via Published with Love

Paperback: ISBN 9798877264861

Edited by Rowan Maddock
Cover Art and Illustrations by Marianne Lang

PUBLISHED with LOVE
www.publishedwithlove.biz

This book is dedicated to Jack and Saskia – you will always remain in my thoughts and prayers.

Contents

VERY GOOD LIVES

Nearly a decade ago, I was searching for a book to be given as a thank you gift to a business leader who had encouraged my work. He was a maverick who helped millions of people secure jobs, with a global impact on giving, education, leadership and charity. But to me and my friends he simply cared, listened and gave of his time – which is often the greatest gift of all.

James was a graduate of Harvard Business School, and I happened to stumble across a small but mighty book written by JK Rowling which made the perfect gift. The book in question – a small, illustrated delight titled *Very Good Lives* – documented a speech given by Rowling to Harvard graduates on the importance of imagination and the fringe benefits of failure. In following years, I would go on to use that book to help nurture future leaders and reach some of society's most broken people, myself included. In many ways, I think this powerful narrative played a part in my progression into the role of leadership fellow at St George's House, Windsor Castle between the years of 2017 and 2018. It certainly gave me the courage to step away from several other aspects in my life and make my own path. Having now read it and faced my own demons, I understand why JK Rowling so often written about dementors and the magical battle between good and evil.

Before politics and power got in the way, I always wanted to change the world. In time, I came to realise that words can either empower or destroy; promote truth and justice, or project it into another realm. I know that the pen is mightier than the sword, but those who say words can never harm you are wrong.

That being said, one of my personal favourite mottos is 'What doesn't kill you makes you stronger'. Whilst it is a cliché – and not always true – I have often found it to be for me. This is why the importance of imagination and fringe benefits of failure have fascinated me so much. More importantly, this is why I have finally lain my sword down and picked up my pen, beginning to write again.

A decade after buying my first copy of *Very Good Lives*, I never expected to find myself working as a bookseller in the same bookshop that sold me JK Rowling's book, let alone using the idea of turning a collection of short texts into my very own series of books called *Published with Love*. These books might not change the world, but I hope they play a part in changing somebody's world – if only for one moment in time. Because, when all is said and done, the moment before us right this very second is all we truly have on this journey of life.

ORIGINAL SIN

By now, if you've been paying attention and reading between the lines, you may have realised that I have walked with some of society's most broken people. I have been a leader, reader and bookseller, all the while empowered by the kindness of others and intrigued by the fringe benefits of failure. Throughout these various turns of life, I have held on to the power of imagination, which allows me to picture a better world and strive to lead a very good life.

This sounds so simple, but as the saying goes, it's wise to never judge a book by its cover, nor an author by their intentions, let alone the final destination of the narrative. To truly understand me, let alone my authority and insight for writing this book, you will have to first reach the concluding epilogue. Just like in life, context only comes at the end of the journey – and with much careful reflection.

But this book isn't about me; it is about my faith in humanity's ability to change, and my sincere fear that we are at the point of no return. It's about the pursuit for justice and humanity in an increasingly unjust world. It delves into society's idea of justice and considers if the word 'justice' itself is a mere human construct, or something actually achievable. Most of all, this book you hold in your hands at this very moment is about who is responsible when things go wrong. Admit it - we all love to push the blame, finding scapegoats at all turns: fate, words, parents, families, teachers, friends and neighbours, leaders, enemies, the media, the devil, our Father in Heaven, or even sometimes ourselves. The list can be endless. Whilst I firmly believe no storm lasts forever, the world is undoubtedly in the middle of multiple storms – and most are of humanity's own making.

Before we move forward on this journey together, I think it's important to touch on the elephant in the room – faith and original sin. Whilst this book may touch on religion, and I unquestionably do believe in a creator or God – or a Father in Heaven – I would like to emphasise that this *isn't* a book specifically about religion. It's a book about humanity and justice. Besides, I am often not much a fan of organised religion, as it can so often be anything but faithful and just. In many ways, I hope the narrative before you helps to challenge the sometimes ironic twist in the tail and tension between truth, justice and faith, versus organised religion. At times, I may even put theology, humanity and our Father in Heaven on trial, in the pursuit of truth and justice. Rest assured, this journey will take you from Jesus to Barbie, past the creation of the atom bomb, across the globe with leaders who should have simply been comedians or reality stars – or even put in jail. Together, we shall ponder who's really in control.

The question I'd like you to ask yourself right now is this; am I my own man or woman, or simply a passenger with a pen? At times, in my own life, I find the answer can be a little of both.

I'd like you to have one takeaway from this book – by its end, I hope to have helped inspire readers to *always* strive to be more than just a passenger with a pen on this journey of life. Or else, we run the risk of tagging along on somebody else's journey, rather than our own; living someone else's life, dream or destiny rather than our own is simply unjust. It makes us nothing more than a puppet in someone else's hands. I believe that this is why God gave us free will, but our little devil within, and the larger devil outside (metaphorically or otherwise) often tries to take over our lives and prevent us from reaching our Father in Heaven – or peace and goodwill to all, whether we believe in God or not.

This book is for people of faith or none. You see, I'm acutely aware that faith or religion can be like Marmite – you either love it or hate it – but rest assured, I am not taking you on a journey of spiritual enlightenment. After all, just like the rest of humanity, I am a mere mortal and if one is to believe in the concept of original sin, I, like you, was flawed at my point of entry to Earth. Which, if true – how can we ever hope to truly find justice here on Earth as in Heaven, if all of humanity is flawed? Especially with the damning evidence of how we take care of each other and the planet is all too clear.

Now, before we take up our individual crosses and put humanity and God on trial, or not as the case may be, I would like to mention a recent reference to original sin in my own life. You see, Marianne – the incredibly talented illustrator of this book's cover – and I have both been fortunate enough to have worked for one of the best bookstores in the world. Maybe I'm biased. Before I digress too far, when we first considered the title of the book and any reference to faith or religion, we both remembered a popular local title called *Original Sin,* by Matthew Roland Hill. Matthew's book is an incredible true story revolving around a battle with addiction and the author's identity after being brought up in a faith-based family.

As a bookseller, I can say with confidence that nearly all who looked at that book judged it by its cover and title – as we are wont to do. I'd firstly like to say that those who did not take the book home – potentially due to the fact it touched on faith – missed out on a powerful memoir which was beautifully written. Those who did read it, myself included, will have hopefully learned something about the depths of despair we humans can reach when wrestling with these concepts of original sin, addiction and an unjust world (and not to mention the damage of sometimes having faith forced upon you). Which leads me back to the original sin of never judging a book by its cover. After all, where is the justice in that?

If original sin is true and we are all born fallen, how do we pick ourselves up and find our way home, before destroying each other and our beautiful planet? Whether you believe in God or not, over two thousand years ago a man called Jesus gave Christians a roadmap towards that answer; our Father in Heaven, peace, love and understanding. Sadly, humanity and religion often distort or ignore his clear message. When challenged, most Christians will use their get out of jail card and simply say – don't judge; we are human after all. And whilst we are told not to judge lest we be judged, the one thing humanity often excels at is judging everyone and everything. I'd challenge you to consider this behaviour which starts when we are children. After all, the burdens and sins (God, I hate that word; wouldn't 'experiences' be better than 'sins'?) of our parents can often become crosses we bear for life.

TAKE UP YOUR CROSS

Some years ago, I remember talking to a lawyer who used to wear a cross that hung on its side, laying horizontal as though it was being carried to its final resting place on Good Friday. I remember her telling me that we all have our own crosses or burdens to carry, and that's true. I also remember mentoring a young man, already a father, who couldn't read very well and was struggling to make his own life stable enough for parenthood. I remember him asking me what the most important thing I had ever learned was.

This question was so heartfelt that I took some time to consider my answer before replying, knowing that as much in life, as with music, it's the space between the notes that creates beauty; otherwise, all we are left with is noise. When finally ready to reply, I explained the following: if I have learned anything during my fifty years on Earth, it is that all humans are always more than one thing, and we categorise human beings at our peril. When we label anyone, intentionally or not, we often negate who they really are. Human beings are multifaceted and precious, much like diamonds formed under pressure, and in today's society we often look at each other in a one-dimensional way, missing each other's individual light. We might like, love, or respect someone for years, until they say something or behave in a certain way, and we are swift to forget all the good that came before. We define and label them for life. Or, worse still, we allow the people who came before us, or those who still walk alongside us, to define others for us.

The first time I ever really understood just how multifaceted human beings can be was during a sponsored leadership programme, travelling with over a hundred business leaders. I often joke that I have become an accidental leader; my leadership experience is routed in lived experience, not in an MBA. So, needless to say, finding myself sitting alongside the boards of some of the world's largest corporations was a little daunting.

Over time, I came to realise each of these leaders had their own demons, dreams, hidden potential, egos and insecurities. Many loved their families and worked tirelessly to support them. At university, these people might have also wanted to change the world, only to cash in their dreams in favour of an excessive mortgage, corporate charge card and Porsche in the company car park. I don't think people sell their soul as much as lose it in the mundane pursuit of surviving life and thinking what they do or have is who they *really* are.

During the programme, the leaders who could break free of these restraints and find themselves truly unlocked their potential, far beyond their original corporate dreams. We were all on the same wavelength, but connecting our dots often meant looking for justice and potential outside of the box or gilded cages that society or our employers had built for us. This was partly the point of the whole leadership experience – being challenged to step outside of our boxes and normal ways of thinking, and to experience life from other leaders' perspectives, whether great or small. Above all else, we were challenged to learn from our mutual successes and failures; often, recognising the humanity in both success and failure connected our leadership experiences vastly more than we first imagined.

One of the most famous human beings in recent times was the late Queen Elizabeth. People so often didn't see the great lady who existed beneath the crown; the irony of this being that the human behind the crown was vastly more important than the crown itself, maybe something even she forgot at times as she wore the ultimate burden of her life. One Elizabeth was real, the other a mere illusion of power, grace and favour. Both had infinite value to others, but both came with their own crosses to bear. Her personal life and the life of the crown. Imagine carrying the hopes, dreams and aspirations of so many, knowing you had little power beyond faith, soft power, diplomacy, wisdom and the dazzlement of diamonds to sustain everyone's dreams.

Elizabeth managed by becoming a servant leader, using her light to illuminate others – which is possibly the only type of authentic leadership that exists – and that's not to mention being the ultimate diplomat. But even the Queen herself had darker hours. She mentioned having to navigate the injustices of the men in grey suits who so often pulled the strings in the shadows of her castles, governments and palaces. More than once, she saw everything go up in flames, but she also understood that this burning led to change, resilience and regrowth. Elizabeth knew that the phoenix can only rise from the ashes. She certainly struggled carrying the dual responsibilities of parenthood and power. And, like all of us, she came into the world with nothing and left with nothing beyond her faith, soul and legacy – and my God, what a legacy. Few people in history have probably had simultaneous access to so many of life's assets and injustices. Imagine that kind of privilege of humanity and burden of leadership all rolled into one. It was one hell of a cross to bear. Metaphorical or otherwise!

One of the last gifts the Queen was given before she passed away in 2022 was a small wooden cross made by prisoners in Scotland. The wood was taken from old pews, carved, and gifted to her just days before her passing. It was the ultimate proof that light can be born from darkness and no human is devoid of the ability to extend kindness – even when serving time at Her Majesty's pleasure.

The ultimate lesson of the cross is responsibility. Nobody can or should put the words 'justice' and 'crucifixion' in the same sentence in the wider sense of what one human can do to another. That said, the ultimate metaphorical lesson to be learned here is that peace which surpasses all understanding comes from taking responsibility for one's actions; we must have faith that life isn't all about us. Over two thousand years ago there were three crosses, all manmade, and all carried by the men who were crucified, crafted by other men in the name of so-called justice. One man sought peace for all. One man surrendered to himself and found peace, and one man fought for who he was until his very last breath and found no peace at all. Whether we believe in Jesus Christ or not, the lesson of carrying our burdens and surrendering to who we are is profound. Ignoring this hidden truth comes at our own peril. We don't have to physically die to find ourselves, but we do need the ego to die if we are to ever find peace, justice and goodwill to all. Managing the ego and loving one another is the only way to cope with life's burdens, judgements and endless possibilities. And it nearly all starts at birth.

CAREFUL THE THINGS YOU SAY

Many years ago, I became a Samaritan and learned to listen. This journey became one of the most profound experiences of my life, especially the training. I was taught how to close my eyes to the world, the art of enhancing what is truly meant to be heard. Some of the most memorable training aspects included aiming for pain; I appreciate that this seems highly counterintuitive when trying to help a person who is in enough emotional pain to consider taking their own life. However, to understand and release pain, we must first come to terms with it.

The second thing I learned was to *truly* listen – this means not just listening to simply respond with our own opinions. This is a skill I admittedly still struggle with! Another important lesson was that to assume something about someone will make an ass out of you. This is because you can empathise, but never truly walk in another human being's shoes. While the Samaritans training taught me a great deal, listening to people who were beyond broken taught me something equally as important. Nearly all of our demons, beliefs and insecurities are routed either in our childhoods or our experiences throughout life.

There is a quote by Lord Tennyson which I used to love, believing it to be fact, but trust me it's not! The quote is 'I am part of all that I have met'. But the truth is that we are not the sum of our life experiences, even if we frequently think we are. So often those experiences – be them joyous or unjust – do not reflect who we really are at the core of our being. We are far more than what we have experienced in life, a truth we forget at our peril.

One of the most thought-provoking songs I've ever heard is 'Children Will Listen', written by Stephen Sondheim and frequently performed by Barbra Streisand. Its haunting lyrics remind listeners to be careful of what they say and how they act around children, as children might notice. The lyrics go on to remind us of the impossible task of parenthood; reassuring our children that everything will be okay, when we know that may be anything but true. The thoughtful song cautions us that our words and desires for others run the risk of becoming magical spells that can last well beyond childhood. Things heard as a child can haunt or define a person for life and, in my experience, frequently do. As somebody who worked in suicide prevention and mentored many care leavers and young adults in prison, I can assure you that the song reaches the very heart of so many of humanity's greatest problems.

One of the greatest lessons a parent can teach a child is that nothing is black or white. Imagine the wars and disputes which might have been avoided if people were raised understanding this eternal truth. As the song reminds us, be careful of the seeds you plant in your child's minds. Because, if only for a moment in time, children will look to the

21

adults in their life in an attempt to work out how to behave and who they are meant to be.

I vividly remember helping a number of imprisoned young adults to complete their victim awareness courses when the world went into lockdown. In nearly every case, it became clear that most of the young men had suffered difficult childhoods, with most being victims themselves, well before they became defined as criminals.

The pain body is a term described by the author Eckhart Tolle in his workshops and book, *A New Earth*. In its simplest form, it indicates how human beings collect or inherit emotional pain throughout their lives. This pain then becomes like a separate entity or 'pain body' that can run parallel to our real bodies and even engulf or take over our minds and actual bodies, becoming a reactive and overwhelming force. Organisations, families, governments, towns, cities and countries can also have emotional pain bodies.

Many of the young men I worked with didn't even understand the injustice served at the start of their life, and whilst it didn't excuse their actions or lessen their considerable pain bodies, pain bodies which engulfed them and the world around them. As Eckhart Tolle would put it, it certainly broke through the humanity, or lack of, in any of the given situations. And as Eckhart pointed out in his book, "one day we might come to understand and use The Emotional Pain Body as a defence", understanding it's often the pain body, not the person, who commits the crime. This might sound simplistic, but if you've ever worked around young people who've gone off the rails, you might give the concept pause for thought. In my experience, the pain within them is so often the overarching reactive force.

One young man who I worked with was haunted. His mother had told him that he was the by-product of a one-night stand and his father had no interest in knowing him, so the two had never met. He couldn't comprehend how a father could not want anything to do with his son. This young man lived his life like a game of Russian roulette, often believing the cards his parents had dealt him gave him no worth. As a child he'd been told he was stupid, as had many of his peers, and he, like them, often believed it. The truth was that few people had ever listened to him. The things he had experienced and listened to in childhood went on to define his experiences in adulthood. The true tragedy here was that this young man was full of potential and talent, but because he missed so much school, this potential was hidden in a way society often ignores, well beyond our man-made statistical judgements of intelligence. Those depreciating words had power, enough to genuinely haunt him through to adulthood. His entire self-worth had been crafted by the words and actions of others starting from birth. And whilst his story might be on the more extreme end of the scale, its eternal truth impacts so many of those locked behind literal prison bars or metaphorical prison bars of emotion which can sometimes last a lifetime. As the Sondheim song underpins, what a child hears has the potential to create nightmares and negative legacies for life.

I remember a former director general of the prison and probation service saying that if we wanted to help lower the numbers of people in prison, we should start with people in care, who often make up over fifty percent of the individuals who find themselves behind bars. This leads to another observation to ponder; if – as the old African proverb says – it takes a village to bring up a child, is the village or society we live in always doing such a good job? And does the responsibility of a child only reside behind their own front door – how about next-door, down the street, in the next town, country, corridors of power, online and beyond the school gates?

As we look around the world, what exactly are our children listening to, playing, reading or seeing? We might read fairy tales to our children to teach them about good versus evil, or occasionally send them to a faith-based group to learn not to judge and to love their neighbours, but every time they go to school, turn on the TV or go online, they are exposed to far more than they should be – and whose responsibility is that? There is only so much that parents can do to protect children from the storms and experiences that life throws their way.

The one thing parents can do is to affirm that nothing is black and white, and we should all be careful of the judgements we make. The profound challenge that comes with this of course is that judgement is so often embedded into the learning experience of a child, let alone the experiences that come later in life. Be it at home, in school, on the playground, on TV, or even now online, judgement is at the heart of their lived experience and formative years. In many ways, it occurs from the moment a child takes their first breath and carries on until they take their last. So, teaching a child how to navigate that human reality or flaw might be the most profound gift anyone can provide. Many children are taught based on a foundation of judgement and justice, but whose foundation or truth is being taught? And does that foundation often negate who the child really is, or withhold and distort the potential the child has to offer the world?

Never forget that what's just and true for a child might differ under a rule of law, culture, or country of birth. Some of these things might include what they listen to, read, see or experience, as well as food, housing, healthcare, parenting, education, and who they can be friends with or who and when they can marry. All too often, the first and final destinations on Earth are frequently not parallel with the saying 'Justice for all'. Never forget, children will listen, experience and see – and our version of truth and justice will form theirs.

IF YOU DON'T HAVE INTEGRITY OF FACTS – YOU DON'T HAVE TRUTH

If deception of humanity and factual integrity begins before we can walk or talk, do any of us really stand a chance of avoiding confusion, disillusionment or judgement?

I was always a fairly serious child, and one day I came home to deliver a message to my parents that the head teacher wanted them to stop parking in front of the school. This deeply confused my parents as they didn't park in front of the school – we lived so close and mostly walked. Under closer scrutiny, my parents discovered that the head teacher had asked *everyone* in assembly to remind their parents to stop parking directly outside the school gates. This was my first journey into understanding context and that what's heard and said might get lost in translation from one human to another. I assure you that I was only about five or six years old, so the actual concept of context came years later. But on that day, for a few moments in time, my parents were confused about being accused of a parking infringement they hadn't committed. I'd simply relayed the message as a young kid – saying, 'Mum, Mrs... wants you to stop parking your car outside the school gates.' Which brings me back to the point. Context is everything. I mean, just ask a lawyer, judge and jury. What's reasonable about doubt? Just ask a child that's starting to doubt Father Christmas. Even at a young age, when doubt sets in we start searching for the truth above all else.

Every day the world moves deeper into the realms of fake news and twisted facts. Politicians across the globe have risen to power, created laws and entered wars, twisting or withholding factual integrity. They proudly use spin doctors to project a false truth and this extends well beyond the corridors of power. It reaches the media - Facebook, X (formerly known as Twitter) – all the way into our homes, churches and centres of spiritual belief to friends and families and beyond. The problem is this: without integrity of facts and context, you cannot have truth. Lawyers and the law are masters at twisting facts to fit their agenda. Anyone engaged in law understands that's so often the case. Many a time, the lawyer who wins is the most capable at playing with the integrity of facts, fighting to keep details from surfacing or blinding a judge and jury with several carefully curated words. They are the most prepared and convincing on the stand. There's a reason why when someone is arrested they are told that anything they say may be used against them in a court of law. But should law be a game set around survival of the fittest, and most convincing? Often these exceptional legal services are routed in costs well beyond a mere mortal's reach, leaving only the wealthiest to be deemed fit.

Either in criminal or commercial law, people often can't take on power or injustice due to the costs involved, and when they do – as with politics – points so often get lost or distorted in the artful debate of each side. Imagine a world where politics, media, faith and law were built on truth and, not as is so often the case, on a slight of hand and distortion of fact. Imagine politics where each side works together to achieve a goal, and courts stopped focusing on the theatrics, simply sticking to cold hard facts – and by that I mean all of the facts, not just some cherrypicked to play the game. We've created a world where the Punch and Judy debate system and a slick game of suits is at the heart of everything. Justice should never be a game, let alone a game few can afford the chance of winning.

Do we start off innocent or true, or as fallen mortals nurtured by other fallen mortals who are simply trying their best? Most children in the Western world believe in Santa, albeit for a moment in time, but only because we teach them about Father Christmas and his Naughty and Nice list. The problem with this is that, much like truth and justice, given time, the real truth will nearly always come to the surface, and when it does, we are left questioning said false truth and the people who packaged it for us. Even with our parents' truth about Father Christmas, once that trust is gone, a tiny part of our innocence is lost forever. After all, a white lie is still a lie, even if it's used for the greater good and to bring peace and joy. Don't get me wrong, I am a massive champion of all things Christmas and Santa, not to mention the joy it can bring. But once our children discover the milk and cookies have probably been eaten by Dad, Santa isn't going to land on the roof and the North Pole might not be where their letters to Santa ended up, a tiny part of their innocence is forever lost. It's often exposed well before the parents are ready to break the magical myth by friends in the schoolground or older siblings back at home. It's a clever way to also inspire children to be good and challenge bad behaviour – but once again it shows justice, subtle deception, manipulation and judgement all begin at a very young age, teaching children to frame what's good or bad and who's naughty or nice.

This leads me back to why the pen is mightier than the sword; the pen often leaves a trail to be discovered, and history or someone somewhere normally exposes what really happened and why. It might take years or centuries, but the truth has an uncanny knack for rising to the surface eventually. I often wonder if that's why the saying 'justice is mine, says the Lord' might be closer to the truth than anyone thinks. Because even when humanity fudges it, the truth lies somewhere in our collective consciousness of existence.

And whilst you might question the integrity of using Santa to explain distortion of facts, the simplicity is in how far people will go to maintain a story and the subtle risk of losing your innocence once the truth comes to the surface. Humanity, not just politicians and the media, are becoming experts at spinning narratives and airbrushing reality, making everything an emotionally charged event or a forged synthetic jolly high. We've had leaders grow out of reality shows and look where that has taken us. Anywhere but reality, especially so with the rise of artificial intelligence. God alone knows where humanity will end up. Maybe at some point, there will be holographic Santas that can say 'Ho ho ho!' and flick switches so that online retailers produce presents out of thin air. Everything we believe is true to us, if only for a moment in time – even if that belief is flawed, a white lie packaged in gift wrap and good intentions. It took years before anyone believed the world was round, but we got there in the end – and still not all believe this fact.

After all, the truth will set us free and this search for truth has taken us beyond the realms of Earth and towards the explorations of the heavens. To quote Neil Armstrong, 'one small step for a man, one giant leap for mankind'. The privileged few who have managed to reach space and look back on Earth have never been the same again – many finding faith in the expansive darkness of time and space.

One of my friends is a former archbishop of Canterbury and one of the world's most eminent theologians. We were sitting together one day, discussing my thoughts on studying theology with a view to considering moving towards ordination, over a coffee in the Old Palace just yards from Canterbury Cathedral. He said something that confused me at the time, especially coming from a man in his position. He alluded to the fact that studying theology could impact my faith. I don't remember his exact words, as this was well over a decade ago, but hearing a world-class theologian and archbishop say that caused me to pause for thought. In reality, he was adding considered context to my emerging faith.

He knew my faith was deep, sincere and rooted in experience rather than a Bible or the pulpit. Years later I would come to understand that faith and religion are often very different, and man's countless variations and interpretations of God run the risk of missing the point or throwing the baby out with the bathwater – an awful image, but there we are. As I once put it to a former leadership director, it sincerely troubles me that the story of Jesus is metaphorically often car-jacked and sold on the altars of countless car boot sales. Jesus didn't actually say very much, but I challenge anyone to unpick his words of wisdom when considering humanity. I can't always say the same for everyone who's spoken or written about him for two thousand years – and I have no doubt he was trying to save us from ourselves and introduce us to our Father in Heaven.

So, whilst I trust in our Father in Heaven, I sometimes struggle with the integrity of facts delivered by man in his Jesus' name or theirs. But I have enough faith to believe that it's only by loving our enemies that we will find peace that passes all understanding. After all, one person's saint is often another person's sinner. But if our Father in Heaven really exists and loves us, why doesn't he save us from ourselves? Is it because, like any parent, he can only guide us towards the light and away from the darkness? One thing is for sure; at some point, we will discover the truth. Either our Father in Heaven exists or he doesn't, and at our last breath we might just find out he does.

ANGELS AND DEMONS

The more I consider humanity, the more I think it's fairly obvious that we all have a touch of angel and demon in us. We might pretend otherwise, but in my experience it's certainly been this way. When I look behind many so-called 'good' men and women, I am frequently reminded of the saying 'evil only flourishes when good men do nothing.' Likewise, when I take the time to listen to people who have made grave mistakes in life, I often see a level of humanity and understanding that bypasses that of an ordinary person. Of course, I have encountered people who are pure evil, but that's been few and far between, and even then, I am mindful of Eckhart Tolles' take on the pain body. People who create pain are often in pain, and I do believe that a human being can reach a stage of pain where they lose their soul and essence of humanity completely.

During the worldwide lockdown, a friend in my bubble lent me the boxset of a TV series called *Lucifer*. I don't normally like watching anything dark, but something pulled me towards it as the world slowly ground to a halt in 2020. The premise of the show is this: Lucifer has escaped from governing Hell and is now having a hell of a time enjoying life on Earth. But he steadily becomes bored with the hedonistic life. So, he becomes a specialist working to help law enforcement and – spoilers ahead – falls in love with a female detective. Whilst falling deeper towards love, he tries to fight who he is to become a better person, all the while struggling against the pull back to Hell or his overwhelming darkness. Whilst Lucifer does do a lot of good, his mischievous and decadent side runs perilously close to the surface. Some of his demonic friends have followed him to Earth and they watch his back as he attempts to find his humanity and fit into life on Earth. At first, he hides his true identity from the female detective, but when his pain body and rage come to the surface, she sees the devil inside emerge.

Whilst this programme is entirely fictional, the reality of watching someone fight the devil within was a profound experience for myself, and it underpins that humanity is rooted in unconditional love. It was also a clear reminder that even Satan, or the devil, was a fallen angel thrown out of Heaven. So, my point is, if we are all impacted by original sin and fighting a spiritual battle – real or metaphorical – striving to purge the ego, demons and the devil inside is part of the journey of finding peace, love and the angel within.

I think the best words that can underpin this are written by the former slave trader and abolitionist John Newton in 'Amazing Grace', who underpinned that he was once blind but could now see. Slave trading remains one of the worst things one human being can do to another. Whenever I consider any word in the history of mankind, I am mindful that 'grace' is the most amazing of words. Its meaning is usually defined in Christian terms as 'underserved favour'. Grace cannot be earned: it is something that is freely given. We count God's grace and the bridge he built in our relationship with him. 'Amazing Grace' highlights how we can be lost and blind to the world and our own actions, but can find grace and clarity of vision through faith and understanding. It takes grace to truly forgive; it takes grace to be a real parent and friend, and it certainly takes grace to be an effective leader. But there is no question in my mind that grace and purging the ego is the only real way to expel the devil within – in search of the angel that could be, and a route back home.

Never forget that even the most patient of parents can crack under pressure, if only for a moment. Pain, fear and exhaustion or excessive pressure can bring out the darkness within. It's only through this pressure that we really find out what's inside, whether that is the formation of a diamond, or the squeezing of an orange.

SQUEEZING THE ORANGE

I was once hurt badly by the church when I had cause to speak up about a vicar who wasn't conducting themselves in a manor becoming a so-called man of God. At that moment, I saw the more human side of religion kick in to protect itself. God flew out of the window, and the man-made machinery that sometimes protects the church put me under more pressure than anything else ever has in my entire life. This wasn't because I was inexperienced in tough positions, even those of my own making, or at the hands of others. This situation attacked my faith and hurt my emerging soul to its very core. It took me a long time to forgive the church and understand my pain, and in some ways although my faith stayed strong, my position around organised religion and trust in people never really recovered.

Oddly enough, the man who helped me forgive the church and come to terms with the pain was a former Doctor of Psychology, Dr Wayne Dyer. He has written countless bestselling books and was fondly known as 'the father of motivation'. His first book, *Your Erroneous Zones,* was written in the 70s and has sold over 60 million copies. It is still in print to this day. The book focuses on helping its readers to navigate negative thought patterns. It basically helps us human beings understand why we become 'messed up' in the first place and goes on to help us consider living life on our own terms.

Dr Dyer also did a lot of public speaking and used to bring an orange onto the stage when he spoke, highlighting the metaphor that when something is squeezed, only what's inside can come out – be that love, patience, trauma, frustration, jealousy, anger, or even hate.

Wayne's personal story resonated with me as he had grown up in care when he was young with one of his brothers, shunted around many foster homes in the United States. He learned from a young age to live a self-actualised life, which interested me as he could so easily have turned out to be one of the young adults I had gone on to mentor, young men who never knew their fathers or had shockingly poor ones as role models. I was fascinated by Wayne's journey, faith and determined spirit. He also underpinned his entire career on the moment in time when he forgave his father. He'd stood over a grave talking to a man he had never met in life. He called that experience 'his greatest teacher'. I would often recall this story to some of the young adults I worked with, especially those who had a parental rage burning inside their lost souls.

Wayne often commented that he saw various families living out their own versions of faith or none whilst he was shunted around foster homes, and it helped him to separate his faith from any one organised religion whilst respecting people of all faiths and none. He had a profound faith in God and his journey certainly went on a spiritual arc of no belief to faith, as he grew to become a parent of eight children.

He often proudly called himself a 'scurvy elephant' after once mishearing a teacher call him a 'disturbing element' through a closed door. Wayne understood the power of forgiveness and the ability to face the fact that what is inside will come out when pressed. He was taught by the renowned psychologist Abraham Maslow who created the Maslow's Hierarchy of Needs. Those needs focused on physiological needs, safety, love and belonging, esteem and self-actualisation.

I'm mindful that when we look around the world – be it in care homes, prisons, war zones, families, schools, front line staff, churches or hospitals tackling emotional wellbeing and trying to help the hardest to reach – many of those needs are not being met. The more our brothers and sisters are squeezed in this life – if we don't find better ways to help one another, nature and the planet – the more the world will be engulfed with pain. So many of the things that squeeze us are man-made, and if we squeeze humanity or the planet too much, there is only one possible outcome.

THE QUEEN'S GAMBIT

Have you ever considered why life often feels like a game, or survival of the fittest/most strategic? Human beings are masters at playing games with each other, strategic or otherwise. One of the youngsters I was mentoring once asked me if I played chess, and I half joked no, going on to quip that any game involving bishops, pawns, kings and queens wasn't for me. But whilst I don't play chess, I can see the strategic similarities humanity uses to get control of the board by removing the lower pieces first, whilst protecting the epicentre of power on the board.

In chess, the Queen's Gambit is a move designed to secure control of the centre of the board. It's one of the most common chess openings and involves white sacrificing (that's the 'gambit' part) a queen-side pawn (the 'queen' part).

From the beginning of time, we are exposed to both games and sacrifice. In childhood, children are taught to share if they want to win friends, letting go of something for the greater good. They also quickly learn how to acquire something or get their way by manipulation or pure force of will, which sometimes involves, rather frustratingly, kicking and screaming until they get what they want.

We are taught in Christianity that God sacrificed or gave his only son to win back control of light over darkness. God is meant to have given his only son to save humanity from themselves or sin. But that poses the larger question of why everything is a game; why is the saviour of humanity included within the parameters of a strategic game or spiritual battle? Games often begin and end when something goes wrong, or when one person strives for control over another, be it on Earth or in Heaven. In many ways, if chess was biblical, the parameters of the game would be reversed with Jesus working to take control of the board by protecting the pawns and lesser pieces on the board, turning the centre of power inside out.

Whether we believe in God, Christ and the crucifixion or not, the game of proving eternity and life after death required someone to die before they could be seen to be resurrected. And sometimes to understand the lengths that human beings will go to in order to take control of the board, we are required to see how one human can so easily crucify another in order to win control of what they want. Whilst others watch or stand back and let it happen, we only have to carefully review history since the beginning of time or look around us today; the modern world is full of land grabs and power plays which see human pawns strategically removed from the board – in this case, Earth.

The odd thing is that, through Jesus, God showed humans who they were, only leaving a few rules to safeguard each other, also known as the Ten Commandments. These rules included loving one another, including our enemies, and to not kill. Whether we believe in God or not, the world and man is anything but just – partly because winning the games we play often becomes more important than life itself. If we are to ever save humanity from itself, we all have to collectively lessen the games which we play, or the games which we allow others to play. This brings us back to justice; a complex, human ideal of finding fairness, resolution and balance. Oddly enough, it's either going to be 'thy will be done', or frankly, we are done.

THY WILL BE DONE

When asked how to pray, we are told that Jesus taught us the Lord's prayer, and if we break it down and play by His rules, we may start to see the rules of humanity's games unravel.

One youngster asked me the age-old question; if God is real why doesn't he step in to save people? The odd miracle aside, that's a bloody good question and one I often ruminate on, but I think the answer lies somewhere in the fact that one of the greatest gifts a parent can give a child is choice, or free will. Without it, for better or worse, we are living someone else's life and not our own. The other point is that if you do have faith and believe in eternal life, then our time on Earth is nothing more than a blink of an eye, the experience no more than a brief moment in eternal time. So, in the great scheme of things, does it matter if you live for an hour or a hundred years? I also suspect you can't have light without darkness in the human sense of the word. Everything has its opposite or apposing force; even in science, every reaction has an equal and opposite reaction. Good and Bad, Fair and Unjust, Light and Dark, Old and Young. How can you ever know or have one without the other? – at least on Earth or in human form.

I don't claim to have all the answers or understand, and I have frequently questioned why, if there is a creator and Father in Heaven – the mastermind of billions of planets, including a flower, tree or oceans, and something as incredible as a human baby – he had to reach humanity by showing them at their worst? My only answer is that we sometimes need a mirror to see ourselves and to reflect realities of ourselves and the world back to us. This, in many ways, forms the concept of restorative justice – where the perpetrator is faced with the victim in an attempt to bring restitution and understanding of the pain caused.

Through my historic work with an organisation called Prison Fellowship, I was fortunate to meet a wonderful couple who sadly lost their son through a stabbing many years ago. We first met at a Christmas carol concert where I was giving a reading. Their story underpins the intrinsic power of the Lord's Prayer better than most, in that they chose to forgive and go on to use their story and the death of their son at the hands of another to help in the healing of other victims and perpetrators. They became champions of restorative justice and went into schools, prisons and communities to share their son's story and use his death to bring resurrection and peace to others. The first time I heard their story I was moved to tears, but over the coming years I came to notice that the light in their eyes showed a peace and joy that surpassed all understanding, certainly, of the incomparable pain and injustice of losing their son to knife crime. And whilst their journey towards loving their enemies might not work or be right for everyone, the peace they found only came because of it. They certainly brought profound light out of darkness.

If God does exist, we are simply his children (spiritual beings) having a human experience. It's through becoming human that we so often lose the humanity of spirit in the process, i.e., we lose ourselves to the trappings of life – or surviving it – and sometimes lose our souls in the process. And even if we don't lose our souls completely, they certainly diminish over time unless we die to the ego within.

Our Father, who art in Heaven,
Hallowed be thy name;
Thy kingdom come;
Thy will be done;
On Earth as it is in Heaven.
Give us this day our daily bread.
And forgive us our trespasses,
As we forgive those who trespass against us.
And lead us not into temptation;
But deliver us from evil.
For thine is the kingdom,
The power and the glory,
For ever and ever.
Amen.

JUDGE YE NOT, LEST YE BE JUDGED

The one thing human beings excel at is judging everything and everyone, and for very good reason; it's literally built into our DNA to help us survive. But since the beginning of time, human beings have turned judgement into a game of entertainment.

'Thinking is difficult, that's why most people judge.' - Carl Jung.

The problem with judgement is that it's often distorted without context and focuses on a surface level of superficiality. Judgement also runs the risk of causing confusion, pain and injustice. But it can also help safeguard us; we are often mindful that following our gut instincts can save us from harm.

Judgement is built into the very cornerstone of childhood and parenting. A child's every word, step and growth spurt are analysed and judged – and the parents are often judged by the world and their wife, including over frivolous things like what they named their baby! It doesn't take a child long to understand that its actions will be judged, not only by friends and family, but wider society, especially when they hit school – they are judged until they graduate. Steadily from infancy, we are judged on our interests and abilities, frequently using a system that bases intelligence on knowing facts and figures. There are certainly various forms of intelligence; from street smarts and common sense, to coming top of the class, to emotional intelligence. The moment we judge anyone, we run the risk of negating them and diminishing their true potential in the world.

Today's children have to face vastly more judgement than when I was growing up. Social media now takes judgement to another level. Capitalist adverts manipulate us into buying constantly, lest we be deemed inferior for not having, using, or consuming something which is meant to enhance us in the eyes of our beholders.

Years ago, any bullying and judgements would hopefully be left at the school gates or out on the streets, but now, thanks to technological advancement, they are linked to a twenty-four-hour news cycle of connectiveness – and that also empowers the judgements to expand like a bush fire. And this doesn't only apply to kids – we hardly ever find peace and disconnect or switch off, let alone stop judging the world and its wife.

We turn on the TV, fire up the tablet, phone or laptop – watch the news while scrolling our feeds, listen to a conversation in the street, workplace, school yard or newspaper and someone somewhere is always judging another human being, often in the name of entertainment. The irony is that all too often, one man's truth and judgement is another man's lie or distortion, partly because judgement is often based on perspective – and a lack of context in any meaningful sense of the word. We tell people not to judge, but none of us can help it; we're a species of chronic judgemental observers and interlopers. It seems wired into our psyche.

I used to consider humanity when I worked in a bookshop with over eighty thousand books and helped customers select their books of choice. So many focused on darkness, judgement and the pain one human can do to another. We had sections for crime, true crime, history, politics, horror, biographies, drama, literary criticism, sci-fi and the latest craze of manga – which often horrified me when considering how ill-suited a lot of its content is for young people. Some manga titles are empowering and cleverly written, but many titles left me shuddering at the stupidity of humanity whilst shelving at work. Titles focused on shock value, chaos, violence, mayhem, sex and pain. We even had a book that had strips cut into its cover to signify self-harm, and bestsellers that focused on rape. Even as I write this book and the next paragraph, I'm mindful I am making judgements on the work of other authors, and the contents of my book will also be judged.

My point is, we seem to love judging other people; our egos feed off it, and when we look at the various forms of documents that chart history or various human creations used to entertain us, we have to question our love for darkness, crime, chaos and judgement. I know one thing – if aliens do exist and one day come to Earth to find out about humanity in our libraries, bookshops, online or even glancing at our TV guides, they would think us nuts or profoundly dangerous. Whether in a book or on a TV screen, you don't have to look too far to see murder and mayhem – crime or justice – packaged as light entertainment. And we wonder how the world has ended up in its present mess.

I remember taking a friend who'd grown up in care, now going on to work around the criminal justice system, to an event in London. This event had industry experts and philosophers debating the philosophy of punishment. By the end of the day, I was a little bemused that some very wise people had spent hours debating punishment and had not once bothered to mention judgement. Judgement is at the very heart of punishment, and we forget that at our peril. Society often wants retribution; to respond to a situation with a stick, but rarely is it possible to fix pain with pain. Yes, you need punishment to help protect and create boundaries and safety in a world made up of billions of people, to teach right from wrong from childhood to beyond. However, judging how to best achieve this result should always be delivered with great care and consideration; we want to avoid causing more harm than good in the long run.

Humanity's thirst to belittle, punish, judge and humiliate is partly why so many media groups and publishers make a fortune out of feeding that ever-growing thirst. And political leaders and policy makers often latch on to judgements in the name of greater good – but is it truly in name of the greater good? Can it ever be? The moment we feed off pain and anger, we run the profound risk of causing a cycle of the very thing we are trying to stop.

Thank God most people in society have learned that physically punishing a child is deeply flawed. The problem remains that we are still a long way off understanding the emotional impact of judgements, words and actions – not to mention content – on our kids and adults as they grow, and try to survive and thrive.

God help us; even religion and biblical texts tell us not to judge, but when all is said and done, they also point out that we are going to be judged on our final day. And we wonder why humanity is so screwed up, or why over the years so much evil has been committed in the name of religion and so-called justice. 'Do as I say, not as I do' comes to mind. That said, if parents judge their children as they grow – and children judge their parents as they grow up – isn't it reasonable to assume that, if we do have a father in Heaven, he will be observing and judge us, albeit with unconditional love? After all, don't we consider and judge our creators on Earth as in Heaven?

PLEASE, SIR, CAN I HAVE SOME MORE?

As I mentioned earlier, our parents' journeys and original sin often play a part in defining the trajectory of our lives. None more so than one of my favourite authors of all time, Charles Dickens. It was many years before I would learn about the formative years of Dickens and how that came to influence his books like *A Christmas Carol* and *Oliver Twist*. Charles Dickens watched his entire family be sent to a debtor's prison when he was just fourteen years old. He had to pawn his father's priceless book collection and go to work in a blacker's factory doing manual labour to raise money for his family. His innate sense of justice grew as he watched his family lose everything, get punished and have to rebuild their lives before he had even left his teenage years. He went on to become a legal clerk and court reporter, with a sparing respect for justice and law – or how it was frequently dealt out to the less fortunate. He had a faith in God but not an overwhelming one in organised religion. He once underpinned this sentiment with the statement; 'Dignity, and even holiness too, sometimes, are more questions of coat and waistcoat than some people think'.

Dickens helped humanity to truly explore itself in *A Christmas Carol*, and helped people to value others. He used the power of exploring our past, present and future in an attempt to grow in spirit and become more compassionate human beings. He created *Oliver Twist* when he was a reporter analysing a paper on food poverty. He realised that responding with a simple document wouldn't make people think, so he decided to get his point across into society's psyche and wrote his famed tale, *Oliver Twist*.

I think *Oliver Twist* may be one of the cleverest ways of teaching both unconditional love and why the criminal justice system is often a challenging cycle of trying to rehabilitate the hardest to reach. We see the signs in Oliver Twist; he has a profound self-value when he, unlike others, is empowered to ask for more. We notice how Nancy, the buxom barmaid, tried to take care of the children and Oliver when she passionately sings 'Because he needs me'. We notice how and why children can get drawn into criminal gangs when they have no family or a poor support system. How they can become artful dodgers to survive and thrive, following the wrong influence, but an influence that shows them some attention, rather than going at it alone. But for me, the most profound lesson in *Oliver Twist* is that the titular character is saved because someone is fighting for him, but The Artful Dodger gets pulled back into crime because it's all he knows; he has nobody fighting his cause.

If a book which became a film and musical – that was created decades ago and is branded with the words 'justice' and 'mercy' above a clueless judge – can capture a reality which so many young people have encountered throughout history, especially kids who have no family and run the risks of a dysfunctional care system, we have to ask why society isn't a better parent. Why haven't we learned? And what chance do some kids have, then or now?

I once mentored an amazing young man who had been in care. His mother was a crack addict which forced him into the role of artful dodger at a very young age. In care, he became best friends with someone whose father was doing life in prison. He was once so messed up he played a part in closing a children's home. For a while, he got his life back on track and became a young father with someone he met after they both left the care system. For a moment in time, he was able to lift his life out of the gutter with an apprenticeship, and then one night got dragged back into chaos by going to a party with his best friend. So called 'friends' encouraged him to take drugs and drink; he then got in a car and crashed into a tunnel at high speed after losing control of the car. He was badly injured; one friend lost a leg, and his best friend died lying next to him in the crushed steel of the car. Both young men had parents who'd gone to prison themselves. I supported him when he was completing a victim awareness course and recovering from surgery himself well over a decade ago. I watched him go on to become a talented actor and speak to many thousands of school children, and work with the police and road safety campaigners – and even get interviewed by a world-renowned TV anchor. But I also saw him leave prison and help organisations who raised thousands using his story, only to send him back to a hostel with £30 in his pocket. Not all charity starts or ends at home.

I remember once buying him a coat in the winter and a mobile phone when he was starting out as an actor, living in a hostel. He had countless bumps on his journey towards redemption and fortunately found a way back to harmony with his mother before she passed from cancer. He became a good father and turned his life around after being a modern-day artful dodger. The question is why he made it and so many others don't.

The answer? He had a good heart. Lots of people fought to help him during and after prison, myself included in some small way, I hope. That young man embodied the story of *Oliver Twist,* and around the world we have lots of young people who fall between the cracks of parents and a broken system. They all have potential, but most who make it have enough awareness to ask, 'Please, sir, can I have some more?' and I've never seen anyone do it alone. People change when somebody somewhere believes in them, and that somebody helps them to believe in themselves. *That* is unconditional love and it's the only thing I know that can genuinely overpower evil or mistakes.

MAMMA MIA

Two of my favourite films are *Mamma Mia!* and *Mamma Mia! Here We Go Again*. The films may be clichéd, but they are fun and rooted in friendship, parenting, potential, sorrow and joy. The first film charts the story of a young girl who's about to get married and doesn't know who her father is. She finds her mother's diary and learns that her father might be one of three men her mother had a brief relationship with when she first landed on an island in Greece. In it, we notice how the mother loved each of the men for parts of their character traits but clearly one man was the love of her life. We learn a misunderstanding kept them away from each other for nearly two decades. So, whilst unsure who the father is, the young girl invites all three potential fathers to her wedding. The films are musicals set around the music of ABBA and start off with the lyrics that remind us that the young woman has a dream and something to sing to the world. Regardless of our start in life, we all have dreams and music within us.

The film is rooted in friendship; the mother has two friends, and the daughter has two friends, all who are very different in character, but the bond and support are clear to see. The old saying that 'you discover who your real friends are when you're in trouble' comes to mind, and in my experience, never a truer statement can be made. I also think a human being's journey can be partly defined by the people we bring into our lives, whether, as the saying goes, it's for a reason, a season, or life.

Amazingly, nobody judges the mother for having a child out of wedlock, something society and the church did for more years than I care to remember, claiming a child was illegitimate or a bastard, two labels that helped define and shame generations of mothers and children all in the name of religion and goodwill to all men. Fortunately, at least in some parts of the Western world, that sense of shame has rightly been replaced with the joy of the potential held within any child. Not to mention the admiration for the strengthening of character and resilience it takes to be a single mother. Throughout time, single mothers have often gone at it alone and done an amazing job, but many gave up their children because of the labels unfairly placed on them by society and religion. And trust me, no matter how great adopted or foster parents are, if you've worked around care leavers or known anyone who's been adopted, that innate sense of who your parents are on Earth (or in Heaven) is always resting somewhere in the background.

One of the most thought-provoking parts of the film is that the young girl meets all of the potential fathers, or dads, as she puts it, and there is an instant bond of love between them all regardless of genetics. Each man comes to think of her as their daughter, happy to have one third of such a special girl. Likewise, the girl loves them all and comes to think of them all as her fathers. If we extend that premise to what so often happens in divorce or real life, we are often shown parents pulling their children emotionally in two in a vain attempt to cushion their own egos and pain bodies, leaving a legacy of pain and injustice that can go on for decades. Real love comes without conditions – this is what makes it unconditional.

Any human who has placed judgement on a child or tried to form their own form of justice around that situation and their birth has left a legacy that diminishes both sides. Fortunately, history has lessened the way a child's start in life is labelled, but around the world it's still an issue in many cultures and religions. And as the saying goes, if you're not part of the solution – you're definitely part of the problem. All life is precious regardless of who the mother or father is.

Mamma Mia! is clever in how it underpins the spirit of humanity to rise through adversity and sustain friendships, but it also underpins how children who are loved unconditionally always want to find a way to honour their parents' legacy. I've noticed with many parents and children from broken homes that it's never too late to bring restoration and forgiveness. Even the late great author Dr Wayne Dyer learned this at his father's grave when he chose to offer forgiveness to a father he'd never met, and one who had certainly failed him before, during and after birth. Wayne's greatest teacher was forgiveness and unconditional love. It brought him the power to surrender and move on. So often a parent or parental figure is much more than a mother or a father; anyone can be a mentor or role model. Forgiveness undoubtedly helped Wayne to become a better father himself, and it's a gift anyone can give to another human being. That said, the innate question of who we are is in our DNA, which is why so many of us wonder who the creator of humanity really is. Because the one thing for certain is that we are one family made up of billions of people. Even if we so often forget that, sadly sometimes for an entire lifetime.

IT'S A RICH MAN'S WORLD

Mamma Mia! Here We Go Again – yes, ABBA were right when they highlighted that it can so often be a rich man's world. And whilst it's true, money can't always buy your happiness or ultimate health – as Steve Jobs, the founder and creative force behind Apple, found out when he became terminally ill – but it can give you power, dignity and choice.

I've had the privilege of walking with some very wealthy people and some of society's poorest human beings, and whilst it's certainly true the wealthy have more options in life, I have also come to understand at times why Jesus said getting into Heaven was harder than a camel going through the eye of the needle for rich people. I think that's partly because so many people think their power and money, and the fruits of it, become who they really are, and often run the risk of losing part of themselves or their soul – which is all we really have – in the process. Don't get me wrong, not all wealthy people lose themselves. Many do infinite good because of it, but so often in life when you really look, it's the people with the least who often give a proportion of the most to the world around them.

So often families with very little are vastly happier than families with so much, who often fight over the finances and almighty dollar, sometimes scrambling for the power of succession and control. Certainly, in my most challenging moments, it's often been the people with the least who have stepped forward to help the most.

That said, one of the greatest gifts we can teach a child is financial stability and the value of money. In my day you might have had a piggy bank or post office savings book, but these days as I stand at the counter of my bookshop selling books, I notice parents teaching their children the power of tapping a card and entering a pin. Nothing is more inspiring than a child who wants to make their first purchase on their own. Many now have their own little debit cards that allow Henry or Henrietta to go get what they want with their pocket money. Some leave me smiling as they decide to pay using cash; it's still a thing for now! As they try to figure out the notes from the coins or make and review change, it's a reminder that money management starts at a young age, be that good money management or bad.

So often children will come in to buy a book, game or gift with their own savings and you quickly understand the experience or purchase has a deeper intrinsic meaning to them when they use their own money or savings. Some parents are wise enough to teach children the power of working for a living or saving. Without question, helping to start a savings fund for a child at birth and empowering them to understand its innate value, and feed it as they grow, will give them choices later in life.

Having everything given to you in life often leaves you unsure of how to live independently and successfully. The old parable of giving a fish versus teaching how to fish is certainly a solid foundation in helping a child to grow up considering how to think and grow rich. And for any budding parents or teenagers considering that very point – one of the greatest books of all time on this concept is *Think and Grown Rich* by Napolean Hill. Its pages help you delve beneath what it takes to live a rich life, and whilst money can give you power and stability and a great start in life, after reading it you're left understanding anyone can create a mastermind alliance, with a definite purpose to succeed in life – anyone. Unless another human being is in control of their life. Which is ultimately the secret.

The justice or injustice of this is a parent can only teach what they know to be true or understand themselves – or care enough about to discover. So, whether it's a piggy bank or Go Henry card, or buying a copy of *Rich Dad Poor Dad* – another great book! – helping a child to manage money and save may be one of the greatest gifts a parent can give.

TRUTH, JUSTICE AND LIBERTY FOR ALL

I remember someone asking me why I brought faith into the concept of what humanity and justice was – and chose the title *Justice – Our Father in Heaven*. So, I pointed out that so often faith, God and religion are placed at the heart of justice and the rule of law, justly or otherwise! From my observations, nearly all of our demons and power struggles, emotionally or otherwise, start in childhood. When recently selling a baby book to an expectant mother, I also considered the following; what world was their baby being born into? Would there even be a world here for much longer? If we were to ask a political leader those exact questions at a public enquiry, they genuinely couldn't give us a truthful answer – no matter how honest they were – beyond the reasonable doubt of 'I simply don't know'.

For many years, when someone gave testimony in court, they used to be asked to swear on the Bible. 'I promise to tell the truth, the whole truth and nothing but the truth, so help me God.' Maybe Lady Justice needed to be reminded of the importance of the truth three times before she could be assured of actually seeing it displayed before God. Or maybe those words have been crafted into a statement knowing that human beings on all sides are often skilled at giving a version of the truth, not necessarily the whole truth, so help them God, whether that be on the stand or in life. Certainly, what a judge or jury often sees is a version of someone's truth – not necessarily the truth – frequently distorted by lawyers, and they must figure out our real truth, justice and liberty for all. The reality – especially when Lady Justice is blindfolded in a symbolic attempt at being unbiased, not to mention the multifaceted elements of humanity – often has a far louder and more complexly loaded gavel than truth before God or man, or otherwise.

Truth, justice and liberty for all is a wonderful tagline or simple mission statement, but beyond those words, is it really true or ever possible? Humanity is made up of billions of people with differing characters, thoughts, feeling, perspectives and opinions.

Beyond the fact that humanity is often a political beast at home, in the office, school, media or wider society, I've tried to not make this book political, partly as I don't really like politics and after knowing many politicians personally and professionally for several decades, I've come to understand that the role, political party and label is completely irrelevant – whilst the character of the man or woman means absolutely everything. Personally, I think many politicians do start off for the right reasons but the culture that engulfs the halls of power around the world so often ruins the best of intentions – and ego, power and position take over from the common goodwill to all humans. And so, the cornerstone of why they started off in politics is swiftly replaced by the power play or wanting to stay in office and wanting their own way, often at the expense of another human being. As one major business leader once said to me, politicians are a rare breed. The irony being that his brother was a member of parliament was not lost on me.

I certainly respect that the role of politician is often a poisoned chalice; it's almost impossible to keep all the people happy all of the time. And the general public hardly ever has to see the entire bigger picture or look beyond their peripheral vision. Therefore, sometimes influencing change, holding the tide and not getting crucified by the other side or your fellow colleagues is the best you can hope for in the house of cards we call political power. But I think the best statement any politician can remind themselves of at daybreak and again at sunrise is that evil only flourishes when good men (or women) do nothing. Then you might not get truth, justice and liberty for all, but you will help to hold back the darkness that seems to engulf the world and corridors of power – so often in the name of truth, liberty and justice.

But the statement they should tattoo on their soul when they take an oath of office is this; so help me God, individually, we can do a lot – together we can do everything. And it would be great if they try to mean it. But that statement should also be embedded on the soul of every human being if we are ever to get close to truth, justice and liberty for all. Or find a way to keep humanity safe and well on Earth.

ROYAL MAIL

The mail we receive, royal or otherwise, can bring moments of joy or moments of fear. I remember more than once receiving letters which hurt me or impacted the course of my life. I also remember opening letters which brought peace, joy and understanding, reminding me that someone, somewhere was thinking of me. The mail is only a vehicle used to deliver the messages of men or women. But its contents have a vast impact: they can bring confusion or understanding, heal or hurt, create or destroy, condemn or pardon, blame or forgive, ask or explain, belittle or empower. A tiny envelope and its contained piece of paper prove why so often the pen is mightier than the sword.

Several years ago, I helped to guide and mentor a law student who was finishing off her degree. I introduced her to key leaders and people working on the front line. I even helped her to review an application to work in the United States during the summer to oversee wrongful convictions and cases on death row.

Fortunately, the United Kingdom doesn't have the death penalty as a form of justice anymore, but several countries do, believing the proverbial eye for an eye is the only form of justice. The problem with this is that, when you work on the principle of an eye for an eye, you run the risk of the whole world becoming blinded by rage – metaphorically or not. You also run the risk of taking the lives of innocent people. I know one man who was sent to prison for murder before his conviction was later overturned. He went on to be an investigative reporter and create a Netflix TV series on the world's toughest prisons. All too often, we hear of miscarriages of justice around the world. It's not a rare occurrence. Therefore, we should never forget that the death penalty doesn't afford any resurrection – at least not beyond biblical terms.

But wrongful convictions also take years to overturn and cost vast sums of money, frequently beyond what the average Joe can find. People caught up in this emotional and legal minefield have been tipped over the edge and some have tragically taken their own lives after being engulfed in an emotional storm they couldn't endure.

When I was born, I actually lived above a post office and local shop as my father was a sub-postmaster before going on to become a serial entrepreneur, master baker and multi-award-winning business man. So I know first-hand that a local post office is often a lifeline and community hub that offers a profound service. I remember my grandfather making me a model shop and post office for Christmas one year so I could play and emulate the family business; it must have taken him months to craft each detail and I loved it, playing at following in my father's footsteps. One of the largest miscarriages of justice in the UK impacted a number of sub-postmasters and sub-mistresses. It took years to discover an IT error was the culprit but, during that time, people lost their liberty and livelihood, or worse, they were blamed and prosecuted for something they hadn't actually done. Many are still waiting for their wrongful convictions to be overturned. The injustice and reality of their situation was bad enough, especially the complexity of trying to overturn a conviction, but the years of fighting to try and secure compensation for an experience beyond comprehension was vastly more challenging than it should have been.

A recent TV drama, *Mr Bates verses The Post Office*, has brought this travesty of justice to the forefront of the general public's mind across the United Kingdom, with everyone calling for a swift resolution and immediate compensation. Not to mention for the wrongful convictions to be overturned or pardons issued. The additional tragedy in this case is that many people have passed away, long before receiving the justice they deserved. And as much as the media is now helping to secure justice, I very much doubt many journalists will sincerely apologise for condemning the innocent when the Post Office first placed the men and women in the dock to be reported on for false and misleading allegations. Not everything reported in the media is always true when it comes to a criminal conviction, or any news story for that matter. So many of the former sub-postmasters and postmistresses were condemned in the courts and on the streets by their own communities, with clueless members of the public spitting at them in the street. Reminding us of the profound truth in 'judge less we be judged'; miscarriages of justice do occur, and the fight to prove one's innocence isn't always as simple as it might seem. Even when the world, or somebody in the shadows, knows you're not guilty.

The Post Office scandal has now led to a major intervention from the government who are seeking to find a way to honour the victims of the scandal and quell public outrage following the TV drama. This proves that the government can move quickly if the tide of public opinion puts fear in their bellies. That said, as anyone who has been wrongfully convicted or placed under arrest for a crime they actually didn't do understands, justice is often hard to find as you fight to clear your name. Individuals who stand accused because of false or misleading statements of others know all too well you can never truly find justice or peace of mind. PTSD often becomes front and centre of the experience. The ripple effect of standing accused because of others and entering the criminal justice arena, an arena that is often a relentless game of chance in the hands of lawyers, is fortunately something few human beings will ever have to understand or navigate.

The recent government intervention and media scrutiny has led to the criminal appeals process and legal system being put under a formidable microscope, with people questioning if it's really fit for purpose. It is without precedent for the government to intervene in judicial cases and step in to overturn convictions, and at the time of my writing this book, countless legal minds are unsure of the long-term consequences this process will have on the legal system and future routes to justice. I have no doubt that a number of senior civil servants are also having sleepless nights, as injustices on this scale don't happen by accident, and they were either complicit or asleep at the wheel when it came to oversight or briefing government ministers properly. Government ministers who also appear to have dropped the ball when overseeing their departments or asking the right questions.

One thing is for sure; everyone who gave misleading information that led to the injustices and convictions should be held to account. That being said, experience would indicate few will be. The truth will be spun for years to come, with everyone blaming someone else or fudging the facts. As I said earlier, humans love to push the blame. Most likely, only the lawyers surrounding the scandal will profit from the fallout as the game plays on. One wonders if the CCRC (Criminal Cases Review Commission) and Appeals Court will also face sleepless nights over what this situation means to the integrity of their work and wider purpose. That's a question only they can ask and answer. The post office scandal has certainly shown that the routes to justice can take years to secure; they are often far harder to navigate than it should be, often with countless lives and emotional wellbeing ending up lost along the way.

Law and justice are vital for a safe and thriving society, but we must have clear, responsible routes to tackle things when it goes wrong, and transparency is vital. We see it whenever there is an inquiry, like the Post Office scandal or Partygate; they take years and often don't achieve the results they are originally set up for. That's not to say they aren't vital, but sometimes when the numbers don't add up, the reasons aren't as simple as we might first think, which is why safeguards, inquiries, accountability and fair justice for all are so important.

Maybe it's time to look beyond the horizon in the pursuit of how we secure justice.

RELOCATION, RELOCATION, RELOCATION

When I was growing up, you didn't hear of homelessness in quite the same way as you do now. There are different types of homelessness, from someone losing their home, to house prices being beyond what many working on the front-line can afford, to people who fall through the cracks of society and see a cardboard box as a place in the sun. But there is also homelessness we see across the globe, caused by man's desire to implode and destroy homes, streets and cities, all in the name of justice or land grabs.

We certainly need immigration laws, but I'm mindful that the lottery of birthplace of conception is often beyond our control. At a human level, I understand the need for boundaries. At a spiritual level, I'm not sure I feel comfortable that any one human being is more entitled to live, reside, or step onto any part of this Earth than another. I know this is a very simplistic thought process on a planet with billions of people, but the morality of humanity's place on Earth is frequently anything but just, let alone rooted in justice.

I firmly believe that our creator believes in diversity; when we are open to new cultures, we learn, grow and thrive. That said, people are so often displaced through wars, especially in the East, and doors are swung open for some worthy souls, whilst slammed shut for others. As a former Samaritan, I have listened to several people who fall into the category of asylum seeker or immigrant. All are judged by society to varying degrees, and few of us can ever walk in another man's or woman's shoes. However, we need to understand this; what we reap around the world and at home, we sow. Why is it fair to care more for one human being or race than another, simply because as a human being somebody does or doesn't remind us of ourselves?

There are no easy answers, but in a world made up of billions of souls, we have to find a way to help ensure people are fed and watered, and if they are relocated that it's done swiftly, fairly and responsibly. I will never forget what some of the souls talked about when leaving their war-torn countries. As somebody who has PTSD from my own emotional battlefields, I am often left humbled at what so many other people go through. If life is a game, with so many leaders setting the rules of the game beyond our control, we have to find ways to help the most broken, because currently there isn't much justice in it.

I don't have the answers, but I do know that no human being should be considered above another, left without food, water, electricity, or a place to call home. It's a returning back to Maslow's Hierarchy of Needs. Individually, we might do something like provide a tent, food bank or clothes parcel – but together we could do a hell of a lot more. We should especially consider why some people are fighting daily for their very lives, or sofa-surfing with no place to call home, while others have the luxury of buying books about it on Amazon or can purchase a new sofa for their second home without a care in the world.

SPACE, THE FINAL FRONTIER

I have always loved *Star Trek* and the idea of exploring space – the so-called 'final frontier for man'. My favourite series was *Voyager* because they got lost in space ironically by somebody playing God, who threw them into another galaxy. But mostly I loved *Voyager* because they became a dysfunctional family who learnt to live, love and work together, striving to possess lives of character and purpose, whilst finding their own way home. The show brought up ethical and philosophical issues with grace, mischief and considered thought, frequently tackling the complex idea of justice whilst lost in space.

Star Trek gave us the first glimpse of AI – something we are seeing expand at a pace few humans are ready for – and helped us consider the moral dilemma of that. The crew on Voyager made many mistakes being human but tried to ground their humanity in the *Starfleet Prime Directive*, a lesson humanity could certainly learn from. The *Prime Directive* was simply – 'Starfleet is not to interfere with the development of a culture that is living or growing.' The TV series certainly showed that was easier said than done, but it also highlighted the danger, moral considerations and ripple effect of getting involved in other worlds and cultures.

We are currently in a space race, and whilst we have pillaged our own Earth almost to the brink, we are now greedily looking at ways to mine the resources on other planets. We also use space for defence and potential command centres for battles of war, as one of my favourite books, *The Future of Geography* by Tim Marshall, highlights all too well. We use space to enhance communications and explore the hand of man, let alone search for alien life and the hand of God. But we also clutter space with debris much like we do on Earth, and will no doubt turn our aerial space rights into some form of cosmic land grab. But we should never forget that space has also showed humanity at its best, striving to reach for the stars and with competing nations of the world working together in the name of research.

The craziest part of humanity is that we know what we *should* do, we just so often don't practise what we preach. But as the International Space Station has taught us, individually we can do a lot, and together we can do everything. A space race, like any race, runs the risk of winners and losers. Sometimes we have to figure out what races are worth it and adhere to first doing no harm. Space shows humanity at its worst and best, especially when we look back on Earth from space. Isn't it time to strive for the best for all and first learn from our miscarriages of justice on Earth, before they become miscarriages in the heavens and amongst the stars?

We are built on the shoulders of our forefathers, but pausing to consider their journey and footprints in the sand – on Earth or the moon and the seas – is vital if humanity is to survive and thrive. 'One small step for a man, one giant leap for mankind' sounds so great, but is it really, if that leap is left in the hands of men who split the atom?

I often find it ironic that Earth is not that unlike Voyager. A giant rock lost and travelling through time and space, whilst trying to find its own way home ethically, spiritually or metaphorically. We might not reach the stars we want in this lifetime, but we have to shoot for the moon and the stars if we stand any chance of maintaining life on Earth or eternity for humanity.

THE CIRCLE OF LIFE

Growing up, I always loved Disney, but I soon learned that it was often run like a steel fist in a silk glove. Like the mystic behind so many fairy tales and castles, there is more than one story behind any myth or brand. That said, it has certainly brought considerable joy to billions and been at the very heart of teaching children the moral high ground and right from wrong. It certainly enhanced my childhood, and I never forgot the first time I stepped into the Magic Kingdom or saw *The Lion King* both on stage and screen.

So, imagine my surprise when I went to see a modern adaptation of it in the cinema in vivid high definition and 3D glasses. The show was powerful and impressive, but as I left the theatre, I was mindful that whilst the story was still the same from years gone by, the lightening reality that it now delivered bypassed the power of subtlety, to the point that innocence was taken to its threshold for a kid in some of the more intense scenes. When the animals fought, the enhanced realism of the modern age left nothing for the subtleties of imagination. I worry that it may even run the risk of scaring a young child – long after going home to bed.

Content and realism have certainly moved on, but we are not leaving much for the imagination of children, and we are certainly robbing them of their innocence both in subtle and not so subtle ways. We expose children to the realities of life in vastly more vivid ways than we once did, wiring their neural pathways to fire at a faster pace than ever before, never pausing for thought. So, should we really wonder why emotional wellbeing in children is at an all-time low?

The circle of life shows birth, death and creation feeding off itself and each other. Nature's only form of justice is that everything consumes everything else and by definition becomes part of something else, albeit for the greater good and to support the life and environment. But whilst nature does that and wastes nothing, humanity poisons our rivers and oceans, and uses, wastes and consumes vastly more resources than it can replenish in a year. Humanity takes nature and the species to the very brink of extinction and rarely learns from its mistakes.

According to biblical texts, man was given domain over the Earth and all its resources, but we have been shockingly unjust and irresponsible custodians. Sure, at certain points in history that was because we didn't know better, but is definitely no longer always the case. I know it's easy to judge humanity as various cultures try to thrive and survive, but if the circle of life and humanity is to go on, we are going to have to become vastly more responsible custodians. There is a point to be made that responsibility for destruction and the consequences of such is also unjustly bestowed around the world, too. Most animals kill for food, a few for territory or dominance, but humanity kills and consumes vastly more than it needs – often for simple entertainment. The crazy part is humanity knows it needs nature to survive. So where is the logic, let alone the justice in exploiting our natural world to the point of extinction?

And just in case you think I am overreacting, a few years back I took one of the law students I was mentoring to a lecture at St George's Chapel in Windsor, where a former chair of NATO spoke on international relations and touched on the risk of nuclear war. He admitted that risk was high but underpinned the risk to the natural world and environment was even greater. I would like to stress that this was a few years ago; both the risk of nuclear war and the circle of life coming to a natural or unnatural end at the hands of man grows by the second, not by the years anymore. Considering that now, I would hate to hear his thoughts on the current state of things.

PEACE, DIPOLMACY AND ETHICS

This lecture at St George's Chapel in Windsor was one I attended when I was a leadership fellow. I actually attended more than one on ethics, and I'll never forget one of the diplomatic speakers mentioning that ethics isn't always the primary thought for a diplomat. Which was certainly food for wider thought.

That said, peace is often forged out of little more than a whim and a prayer or diplomacy at its best. St George's House, which is attached to St George's Chapel, is a centre for leaders to come together both of faith and non-faith, with the society of leadership fellows being created to nurture leaders, offer support and create considered debate. It frequently runs leadership conversations with its members to find ways to enhance leadership at home and abroad, whilst aiming to tackle some of society's and the world's most challenging issues.

Whenever I think of peace, I think of the Biblical saying 'the peace that surpasses all understanding', partly because I think peace can only be found when diplomacy is at work, and an ethical stance is considered. But for peace to flourish, often various differences, wishes and objectives have to be blended, or conceded, or worked out for the greater good. Which is often harder said than done. Creating conversations is by definition the blending of more than one voice.

From time to time, most of us are diplomatic and would rarely say all we think to another person. We craft our words hopefully with care and consideration in an attempt to take people on a journey with us. A book which showcases this is the classic *How to Win Friends and Influence People* by Dale Carnegie. The book was written years ago but its gems of wisdom are still very much valid today, in part because whilst humanity evolves, human beings often remain intrinsically the same in the way they think and operate. Most people like to be listened to, loved, or at the very least valued and respected. At first glance the book is fluff without much substance, purely promoting common sense – but its wider integrity is much greater than that. It's certainly a book every child should read in school, or at least a book everyone should read once in their life.

The weird thing about humanity is that often the simplest answers are the best. We make life vastly more complicated than it needs to be. Because of the stories we tell ourselves and each other, we often let the narrative become so distorted and full; we run the risk of not seeing the wood for the trees. I remember the author Jeffery Archer sitting with me in his penthouse overlooking the Palace of Westminster and saying writing the book was easy, but the editing process is the challenge and the most important part, and trust me, some years later I would agree. And whilst I may be writing this, vastly more talented people than me will edit it, if only so you can diplomatically see the wood for the trees. Which is also a good analogy for our life; if we are to succeed, we must keep editing our lives, stories and words.

If we are ever to have peace on Earth, we have to understand our words are a priceless part of that journey. They can so easily cause resentment, destroy and disempower, but they can also build up, restore and bring peace, understanding, enlightenment and goodwill to all. That said, as an avid reader and now a writer, I come to understand the energy and intent behind our words is often just as important as the words themselves – if not more so.

Remember the old saying – 'You might forget what someone says – but you will never forget how what they said made you feel'.

HEAR ALL ABOUT IT

News, media and social platforms – the whole world's got an opinion, and we're constantly forced into hearing it. When I was growing up, there were not that many ways to get the news, but that has changed at a lightning pace. These days anyone can publish a blog, write a book, post an update or add a comment. The world is full of news men and women, both skilled and unskilled. Technology has unlocked humanity and I'm afraid it has given the concept of free speech and news a whole new meaning. So, with artificial intelligence coming down the road at lightning speed and more spin on the web than any spider could possibly consider making in a lifetime, we have to be sure we don't get caught out by the media web humanity has created for itself and each other.

Don't get me wrong; the media, a well-considered post and a talented journalist can save lives, empower and bring profound understanding, and many journalists put their lives on the line to report truth and justice. That said, so much of the world's news content has been emotionally charged to capture its audience in a grip humanity barely understands, or turns news into entertainment albeit in the name of current affairs.

The first person to really encourage me to write used to run one the world's largest news outlets. I remember him sitting me down and us having a Charles Dickens moment that mirrored *A*

Christmas Carol as I considered what my story had been, what I wanted my story to become and then creating a roadmap to get there. I remember thinking I knew what my story had been, but I had no idea what I wanted my story to become, so any roadmap I built couldn't really get me where I wanted to go. So, I let circumstance and the ideas of other people define my journey and direction. Which, if many of us are honest with ourselves, we frequently let other people determine our thoughts, journeys and beliefs.

I certainly came to understand that one person's – one country's – account of news might vary from another. One journalist's point or pivot of justice might not be another's. So many news outlets are underpinned by a political or personal agenda, or commercial tailspin, or bias that we as consumers might not even be aware of.

I remember the former news executive and director of journalism helping to guide my thoughts on an article I was writing, and he cautioned me to craft two versions of the same story, one for broadsheet press like the *Times* and another for the tabloid press like the *Mirror*. Both stories were about the same subject matter, but the context and delivery were altered to engage the reader depending on the publication. One became lighter, edgier and funnier than the other, but both wanted to engage the minds of the readers in the same way. He also taught me that one clear visual image could tell a powerful story in itself, a point I have never forgotten and certainly mentioned to the illustrator of this book.

However, when I consider the news – and we have to consider all of it, lest it be fake – I am left on one point: if our daily news is curated for us, and it is, and we have billions of people on the planet, which we do, how do we end up with ten to twelve news stories each day that are used to define our world's news across a number of abridged news agencies? It is news, but it's far from world news or a true indication of what's going on in humanity. After all, as messed up as humanity is, there is still vastly more good in the world than bad. It's just that good is not as much fun to report – and it certainly doesn't enrapture readers or listeners' pain bodies in the same way as the emotionally-charged narratives that are so often reported with a base line or fear, condemnation or outrage.

I do know some wonderful reporters; I believe that it is possibly one of the most admirable professions, when delivered with truth and justice. Sadly, this is often not the case. And trust me, our news delivery does impact the emotional well-being of our children, a point recently researched and debated on morning television.

We must always consider our impact on future generations. Remember to be careful with the things you say as children will listen. Be careful with the things you do, print or publish as children will invariably see – it's not always easy for a reporter, parent, reader or child, but we need to clean up our act and move away from news as emotionally-charged entertainment or a politically-charged narrative to help distort truth and justice.

THE RIGHT TO BEAR ARMS

Out of any in this book, this section causes me the greatest concern in the world. In the UK, we have an epidemic of knife crime, and around the US the right to bear arms leaves behind it a trail of empty school seats, with more graves than the world should see.

Every culture has its own ideas of what's right or wrong, but how we've not learned to evolve past the ideals of the Wild West I do not know. No civilised society should want nor need civilian access to hundreds of millions of guns; there are more than the human beings who reside on that cherished piece of Earth. Guns and fighting each other are now firmly built into humanity's psyche. We've done that to each other, we've allowed that to happen – it's our fault. Children play with toy guns, then turn to high-definition video games to see how much death and destruction or mayhem they can create whilst playing with their consoles or virtual headsets. Turn on the TV, flick through your streaming channels, or go to the cinema and there are numerous options to be entertained by watching each other get blown up or killing one another with one weapon or another.

We all have to take responsibility for the way we think about arms and weapons, whether they are currently legal or not, and few countries have got it right.

Recently the world has awoken to multiple wars at the same time with real explosions of destruction unfolding across the globe. In 2023, Hollywood's *Oppenheimer* (Christopher Nolan, 2023) showed us the story of the atom bomb's creation, and how its creator realised the risk to humanity crafted by his own hands too late, only to be politically replicated and used by other leaders who wanted greater power of death and destruction. Defending ourselves is important, but we've created a world which has so many weapons embedded in its soil, floating in our oceans and above our atmosphere, it's only a matter of time before one lunatic actually presses the red button or something gets into the wrong hands – or a mistake happens, and a nuclear weapon goes off by accident. History has already seen plenty of nuclear power shutdowns for us to know the devastation an incident of this scale could cause.

If man's ability to build is exceptional, and it is, its ability to destroy one another and itself is steadily getting stronger by the day – and when we are entertained by weapons, we are part of the problem, not the solution. The madness in this is that few of us can say we are totally innocent in what we consume, whether that is through books or on one device or another, and what we allow our kids to see is not always appropriate. And we wonder why it leads to so many needless deaths; we must not forget the lack of justice in the value of the arms industry. No human really has the right to bear arms in the first place, but I accept it's too late to turn back time completely. Until humanity realises that the genie we've let out of the bottle is vastly more unmanageable than we thought, it's only going to get worse.

Maybe we can't put the genie back in the bottle, but we can start to challenge ourselves on why weapons, death and destruction is part of humanity's idea of great entertainment.

YOU CAN'T PUT THE GENIE BACK IN THE BOTTLE

So many times in my life I've wished for a DeLorean time machine to go back to the future. We all learn from our mistakes and grow, or end up repeating them; this is why weapons of any kind and our lack of respect for them is beyond comprehension. Several years ago, I stood accused of being naïve, and I certainly was. I wanted the world to be better and became passionate about social justice. I was even politically hoodwinked by leaders who should have known better, albeit for a moment in time.

I've said it before, and I'll say it again: this book isn't about me. There is plenty of time for my story, but that's for another day. I've genuinely tried to write this with considered thought, personal faith and any wisdom I might have picked up along the way. This book was never written to change the world, just to wake humanity up a little about why everything we do around children determines their journey and the destination of humanity, especially if you believe children are at the forefront of our future, which I certainly do.

I have faith and pray to God that some miracle will abound and save us from ourselves, because frankly, I don't see how humanity will make it through the storms we create without global pause for thought and a significant change of societal direction.

If I was naïve before, I'm not anymore, and if God is real and placed humanity on trial today, I am sure we would all collectively come up short. Maybe we can't put the man-made genie back in the bottle, but we *can* wake up and smell the roses. There is still time to change the path we have set down. I firmly believe that, much with the rudder on a ship, it takes small defined steps to create sustainable change, and I do believe there is vastly more good in the world than bad.

We can't turn back time, but we can consider each step forward more carefully, and that has to include what we teach our children, how we work together and how we select our world leaders. In recent years, the Western world has picked leaders who entertain first and think later. The one thing we can do is think first and then lead. The golden rule is to love one another as we do ourselves; the only problem with that is all too often we don't love ourselves, so we have no clue about how to love our brothers and sisters – or children across the globe.

I think the creator of the universe did come to try and save us two thousand years ago and I do believe that he left us with a blueprint of how to put the genie back in the bottle, right our wrongs and turn back time. One thing is for certain; unless we follow that golden truth, it is game over – and not just on our PlayStations or Xboxes.

If we truly want to turn back time, our global leaders and our kids need to be taught the pen is mightier than the sword – and maybe, just maybe, have a little faith. As you read on you will start to see that not all is lost; humanity has seen injustices come to the surface and made some steps forward – or at least start to consider what's just in love and war.

PLASTIC FANTASTIC

Every week, I am more alarmed by the level of plastic we seem to use to get through the day. We know that plastic poisons our oceans, destroys ecosystems and fills up landfills to a level which our natural world can barely withstand; this is a fact. We've made tiny inroads but not enough. We seem to think plastic is fantastic as it supports our flourishing disposable culture, but this mindset is an example of ignorance.

This year, we saw the iconic plastic doll reach our cinema screens in the form of *Barbie* (Greta Gerwig, 2023) giving a whole new meaning to the Spice Girls catchphrase 'girl power'. But single plastic use aside, the Barbie doll has done quite a lot for humanity. Maybe not so much in its early days, but Mattel soon came to realise the power in showing women that they can be or do whatever they want. Children learn through imagination, and toys play a profound part in the early learning experience. For a moment in time, Barbie certainly ran the risk of projecting the old stereotype of what the ideal woman was, but gradually, despite being a commercial enterprise, it found a way to move with the times and give young girls – and boys, in some cases – what they wanted. A fresh insight into the diversity of humanity, and especially girls. The possibilities are endless.

Then after decades of fame came the film, which had enough emotional maturity to make fun of itself but also challenge the idea of identity and justice for both men and women. Many women saw it as a rallying cry for just how far their gender has come, and whilst our world seems to get more than occasionally drawn into the plastic and falseness, women are moving outside of their man-made metaphorical Barbie boxes and assuming leadership roles in a misogynistic society, redefining the status of what it means to be a woman, whether one is born that way or not. Not to mention who has the right to wear pink.

We have seen a sea of change in women's rights, most recently through the #MeToo campaigns, and we are now hopefully redefining the games little girls play, whilst broadening the imagination of who they can grow up to be – and what's acceptable in the real world, taking on sexism and women's rights. People shouldn't be defined by their gender or place of birth, and whilst things are improving for girls and women in some places on the planet, there are still countless injustices and roadblocks for females around the world.

In my bookselling job, I have noticed that children often have their own minds when it comes to selecting a book, but that choice needs to be backed up by a diverse and empowering selection of narratives which help the children reflect on how they see themselves – or more importantly, how they could go on to see themselves as they grow.

The games we design for children are an essential part of nurturing their potential, and if a small plastic doll can empower a generation to grow and positively consider the gender roles of the future, we must dig deeper and consider ways to build on this, with media content, books and games that unlock the potential within for boys and girls of every orientation.

Remember, the Barbie film reached an adult generation, sweeping into cinemas across the world in a wave of Barbie-fever, but the viewership interest in all things Barbie first began in childhood. This is a powerful reminder to be cautious around what we say and do as children will invariably listen, see and learn – dreams, whether crafted in imagination or plastic, have the profound ability to be recycled in generations to come.

A VIRGIN, THE WORD AND THE WORLD

One of my favourite spiritual songs is 'Mary, Did You Know?'. It poses the question: did you know your child would save humanity? Did you know that your child might use his hand to calm a storm? The reality is that we will never know what Mary did know, and we simply have to trust in our faith.

Throughout time, people have told us about the Virgin Mary. In the Catholic faith, she is a pivotal figure in the journey of Jesus Christ, just as any mother is in the story of their own child. This book touches greatly on God for those who believe – but mothers are probably the first and foremost part of any child's life; after all, a life cannot begin without a mother. Certainly, that role has been defined and redefined throughout time, frequently and unfortunately with men determining what the role should be or where a woman's worth resides.

Like 'justice', the word 'virgin' is, like many words, pre-loaded with more definitions and misconceptions than any dictionary can bear. It's even been used, or some may say exploited, by business leaders for a brand name or musicians for shock value. Whether you have faith or not, you play around with the legacy of innocence at your peril.

A case in point - whilst some of the imagery and lyrics the legend and singer Madonna has created over the years has genuinely shocked me, and caused me pause for thought (something many talented artists and musicians embrace to make an emotive point), her astonishing talent, voice, passion and support for LGBTQ+ rights - not to mention individual human-beings sometimes on the fringes of society is sincerely humbling. I have no doubt that Madonna's message to people in certain communities has saved a life or two and prevented somebody from feeling quite so alone in the world. Alongside her profound and awe-inspiring journey into motherhood, adoption and philanthropy which has left me inspired. Including Madonna's work to honour her adopted children's heritage. Once again proving we are all incredibly complex, multifaceted human-beings - living our own truth and wonderous journeys. We judge each other at our peril, even if they sometimes offend us!

Over the last few years, women's rights have risen to the surface – and rightly so, after being suppressed for generations. That said, some of our foremost leaders in recent times, including the late Queen Elizabeth, have been women. We have also seen laws change, levelling the playing field as society evolves considering succession. That said, in many places around the world women have more rights over their minds, bodies, babies and futures than others.

In recent years, and partially thanks to the #MeToo movement, the topic of consent has been brought to the forefront of adolescent minds, with people considering what real consent is and the importance of it, especially for young men and women. But as with a number of changes, we have also had to navigate the technology revolution and how that has opened up sex and sexuality to the world at an ever-growing pace. We now must face the facts that many children's sexual education and initial sexual experiences might arise from other children who have consumed adult content far before they are ready and is appropriate. Content that is often dangerous, damaging and deeply distorted.

Innocence is the cornerstone of childhood, and we must find better ways to protect and nurture our children. The first known case of virtual rape has recently occurred in the metaverse – and nobody was prepared on how to handle the situation, let alone where the rule of law applied. Everything comes down to intent, but protecting our children from the real and emerging virtual worlds is a growing dilemma. Parents, leaders and lawmakers around the globe are already begging platform and content creators to put safeguards at the heart of their design and algorithms, pleas which are currently falling on deaf ears.

FROM JESUS TO A CHILD

Whenever I think of Jesus, I think of a child who was born and grew up intending to save humanity. I also think of kindness and of striving to reach society's most marginalised. But when I think of religion, I sometimes think of the distortion and manipulation that has been attributed in the name of faith and justice since the beginning of time, none more so than for people struggling with their sexual identity or labelled gay or homosexual.

For decades, many cultures, including my own, made it illegal to be or practise homosexuality. Many cultures and countries around the world still do. And the frustrating, heartbreaking part of this is its emotional damage and repression upon generations of people. It's a searching issue and in my opinion, at times the church and religious leaders have unquestionably got it gravely wrong, for far too many years. Thank God homosexuality is no longer illegal in the UK, but we have a long way to go; there is still an overwhelming generational prejudice that is beyond soul destroying.

This book is about justice in all senses of the word, and one of the reasons I admire my friend Dr Rowan Williams, former Archbishop of Canterbury, is because he tried as a leader to put across a fair stance for the LGBTQ+ community – in many ways speaking up before the church and wider world was ready to listen. Some even tried to crucify him for standing up for the most marginalised in the LGBTQ+ arena. He learned that pushing on a closed door before it's ready to be opened isn't always easy, but that doesn't make it non-essential. I know first-hand from our conversations that *with reflection* he feels he made more compromises than he wished he had – if only to appease all sides. But as I told him, many of my peers feel he stood up for them when so many church leaders didn't. One thing I learnt while walking with leaders on Wavelength Connect and at St George's House is that it's never easy being at the top. Leadership can often be a very lonely place – you are holding the hopes and dreams of everyone your title makes you responsible for. It's often a privilege, blessing and poisoned chalice all rolled into one. A journey few will ever truly understand.

Faith, law and justice are subjective. Many people have used their faith to interpret artwork or make a profound statement, often with shock value to expand reach, but sometimes to make a profound point about unconditional love and faith.

Growing up, I had close friends in the music industry, and some worked closely with the late George Michael. I watched George, albeit from a distance, face a number of judgements and injustices. Yes, he made mistakes – we all do from time to time, and battles with addictions and walks on the darker side of life often engulf many artists – but he was pressured to keep his sexuality vacuum-packed for a society, industry, world and family that he felt wouldn't accept him for who he was. He became deeply frustrated that his sexuality was bound to his musical talents, and when he finally came out to the world it was with the sorrow of losing a partner and revealing his faith all at the same time. Yes, he had demons to battle until his last Christmas on Earth, but you genuinely wouldn't have found a more generous or kind soul on the planet. Unlike so many self-proclaimed philanthropists, George often gave behind the scenes and with infinite discretion; he was humble, a rare trait to find in today's society.

He gave all the proceeds from his song 'Jesus to a Child' to the charity Childline, something that only really came to the surface later in life. Imagine how many lives that money may have saved. He also battled with commercial law and the rights to his music, going on to try to take on the musical giants Sony, who controlled every aspect of his music. George was so determined to protect the integrity of his music and intellectual property that he stood firm around not recording any music whilst he fought the fairness of his commercial contracts. In the end, he didn't win against Sony and that battle played a significant part on his emotional wellbeing and ability to write, perform and release music. Countless artists have found themselves trapped by recording or publishing contracts, written and signed with little advice or guidance when they were young or just starting out, unable to pay top lawyers to protect them in their fledgling years – or too naïve to even try. The rule of law is often subjective, but certainly not always just, and the legacy of any injustice can seep into our souls, as it certainly did with George.

So often man-made or self-made injustices that last a lifetime are behind our demons and addictions. How society, leaders and religious institutions have navigated LGBTQ+ rights are some of the greatest abuses of power known to man; dictating to someone who they are is fundamentally wrong, and it's nothing more than emotional terrorism.

And if you ever need a reminder of society's injustices to the LGBTQ+ community, pull out a £50 note and consider a man who helped invent the first computer and played a major part in ending the Second World War. Alan Turing was a brilliant scientist, driven to his own death because he was crucified metaphorically and chemically for simply being gay.

TAKING THE KNEE

When I was growing up, you never really thought to question authority or the integrity of a politician or the police, certainly not in the way we do now. But history has shown us that sometimes, when one human is in a position of power over another, they can and frequently do abuse that position of power and trust.

The first time I witnessed racism, I would have been too young to fully understand it. I went to a small private school and several of my friends were from Japan, China or India, and trust me, that was a shock to the system in '70s Wales. I remember going swimming around the age of seven or eight and hearing people shout jibes at my school friends – simply because of their place of birth and colour of their skin. Many years later, while guiding a London school set up for the Windrush generation through modernisation, I came to understand that when I was growing up, history around heritage and identity was often airbrushed way beyond its reality. So often our culture – not truth or justice – defines our history.

In 2020, I think the world saw a sea change around understanding the stark realities of prejudice, institutional racism and abuse of power when George Floyd was killed. But they also saw how an abuse of power can take a life – directly in front of the watching public. And with our phones and social media advances, this uproar had the power to spread like wildfire.

I've had the privilege of becoming friends with men and women of countless cultures, and even helped some leaders from other countries explore rehabilitation and suicide prevention schemes. Every time I've stopped to learn about a different culture I have discovered something profound about humanity and, sadly, man's own inhumanity to one another.

Much like with taking the knee, a cause can be politicised or misrepresented but an abuse of power must never be allowed to flourish; all men and women should be equal. Sadly, in this world they are not, and the legacy of slavery to pillaging nations should never be diminished or left unchallenged. Just like with Black Lives Matter, the true narrative nearly always comes to the surface given the passage of time, even when that injustice is at the very hands of someone charged to protect us.

When I consider my journey with young offenders or my own broad view of justice, I am left with a clear understanding that the people drawn into roles of power are often drawn to them for the wrong reasons. I have many friends who work on the front line, and I know that during recruitment, focusing on the emotional intelligence and rooting out the people attracted to the power over another human being should always be at the centre of the selection process. With power comes great responsibility to do good, or to abuse it.

103

THERE'S NO ROOM AT THE INN

I have already touched upon my profound respect for the work of Charles Dickens. However, the man is far more interesting that common knowledge leads us to believe. Dickens started a home for fallen women long before it was popular to even care or talk about the situation. Not many people knew about his background or that his family ended up in a debtor's prison until after he passed away. I was also interested to know that, according to society's terms, he was one of the first people to come close to what we might call a celebrity in today's world. Not just in the UK, but also around the world and in the United States. Dickens never really bought into the establishment's idea of celebrity, but consistently strove to provide humanity with some self-awareness – also believing and frankly proving that the pen is mightier than the sword.

Much like Charles Dickens, I've also explained that I have a faith in God but am sometimes wary of people of faith and a religion which is so often anything but biblical. When I was living in London well over a decade ago, I wanted to find a gift-giving space for the Angel Tree project, where we could give *prisoners children* a present and faith-based book. I was asked to co-ordinate the project on behalf of a faith-based charity. In order to make room for the initiative, I needed to find a 200 square-foot space available for a few short months, noting that a few thousand books and presents would need to be co-ordinated, then wrapped and shipped as they were donated around the country. I remember reaching out to countless churches and religious leaders at the time, and the response was always that there was no room at the inn. Everyone seemed to love the project, but nobody could find space for it. In the end, I convinced my housemates to convert some space as I was fortunate enough to be living in a Christian community in central London, but I never forgot that all across London, many people who could and should have found space didn't even try.

I've frequently come to understand that walking with society's most broken and the comment Jesus made around 'did you visit me when I was in prison?' is more profound than we think. So often places are open for an agenda but when there is an overwhelming need, even for a child two thousand years after the birth of Christ, there is no room at the inn. Justice is in the eye of the beholder, and not always in the hands of someone holding a Bible.

Don't get me wrong, I have many friends who work in churches far and wide, from lay preachers to former archbishops, and genuinely believe in their calling. I don't mean to be irreverent, but I so often see squabbles over who puts out the Bibles, and sermons delivered with such gusto and gossiping around the pews, let alone emotional manipulation going on behind the pulpits. So, as the Bible said, 'words without deeds amount to nothing'. I know if many churches and religious leaders around the world were put on trial, they would fall short, especially around safeguarding and finding no purposeful room at the inn. This matter is improving in tiny pockets but still has a long way to go, and if churches don't change and make themselves vastly more purposeful, relevant and just, they will move towards extinction.

THE PEN IS MIGHTER THAN THE SWORD

You might have noticed that the *Published With Love* logo is based around 'the pen is mightier than the sword', a profound statement which runs through this publication and the rest to come.

I know you may tire of hearing me say it, but the might of the pen should never be underestimated. It can chart history and inspire – and have a bewildering creative force; as we know, words breathe life and underpin creation.

That said, the old rhyme 'sticks and stones can break my bones, but words will never harm me' is simply not true. Words do wound and destroy, as well as build up and create. If you pause for one moment and look around the room or space you're in, absolutely everything was created for you by someone else, and that all started with words if only in their mind's eye. Even your decision to read this book was rooted in words you told yourself, or words spoken to you by another.

Each and every word in it has been metaphorically chiselled onto the page just for you. I have published this book with love in my heart, and if it's flavoured with judgements, that doesn't mean they are always right, simply observations on the journey of humanity, and my experience of how it abridges the rights of passage of any child, both with their parents on Earth and God.

I know I don't have all the answers, but the book was written with a personal history rooted in Jeremiah 29:11 – "'For I know the plans I have for you," declares the Lord, "plans to prosper you and not to harm you, plans to give you hope and a future.'"

A CHRISTMAS CAROL

I absolutely love Christmas. So much so that if I ever won the lottery, I would buy a Christmas tree farm and live on it in a log cabin with a husky or two, giving away Christmas trees to families who struggle over the festive season. I once saw a Christmas film that helped to sow this idea into my mind's eye. I think the love of Christmas started as a child; my dad used to sell Christmas trees and holly wreaths, so our garden was full of them well before Christmas. I'll never forget my dad looking deeply distressed one Christmas when our new puppy decided to trample all over the merchandise.

I also love the way the public engages with the Christmas spirit. My first job was selling flowers at a pound a bunch in one of my father's stalls in a market over forty years ago, so retail and customer service have always been in my blood. Which is why I have also agreed to return as a Christmas Peak Bookseller to my old bookshop. For me, being around books, people and the Christmas spirit will bring some peace and much joy. That said, I am also mindful that Christmas is about the birth of Jesus, not just Santa, trees and books – and the reason my dad once sold holly wreaths is as profound today as it ever was. Christmas holds memory and power for me, and for this reason I decided to launch my website at Christmastime, with the publication of this first edition from our collection coming in the New Year, in honour of my fathers in Heaven, both human and spiritual. I hope and pray that my own dad is with my Father in Heaven and has eternal peace. I hope you relish in the thought that this book has come from a place of sanctuary and hope.

Charles Dickens' *A Christmas Carol* not only beautifully captures the concept of the human pain body in Ebeneezer Scrooge, but also the kindness that can unfold around the Christmas spirit, bringing light to the world and injecting peace, joy and reconciliation into the family and community.

When the world went into lockdown, I found myself in an odd position as a temporary mentor and father figure to a number of young adults in a prison. It was a deeply challenging wing, and as lockdown began I was asked by one of the managers to help break the news that these young adults wouldn't be getting visits for months and would be residing behind their doors for nearly twenty-three and a half hours a day in an attempt to keep them safe from the unknown virus engulfing the world. The front-line staff, like all front-line staff, put their lives at risk by coming to work each day whilst having to work and navigate their own battles back at home. They were hidden heroes, navigating the world within a world which the public rarely sees or thinks about. Watching some of the young adults' faces as they realised everything was shutting down still haunts me, but I am pleased to report that they got through it. Over the course of multiple lockdowns, by working together, we found ways to engage them, often with reading but also with something rooted in *A Christmas Carol*. considering their own story, their past, present and future – going on to create a roadmap for life.

One of the books I introduced them to was *Very Good Lives* by JK Rowling, which I referenced in the foreword to this book, and a few other titles from authors I knew or respected, many of those titles which I have already referenced throughout this book. I highly recommend you pick them up and give them a go – there is something to be taken from them all.

I also helped them to consider writing their own stories. I often think of the metaphor of prison as a mechanic's garage. Some garages are good, some not so good. You can leave the car in there and do nothing, or worse, give it to a bad mechanic and then put it back on the road and expect it to function properly. Which it won't. Or, whilst it's in the garage, you can review what went wrong, help to repair it with a qualified mechanic and get it back safely on the road. I call this line of thought the CAR Strategy; focusing on Character, Attitude, and Responsibility. A universal image, I use car analogies to help young men understand themselves and their actions. They look in the rear-view mirror, consider the passengers in their lives, the suspension, road ahead and fuel, albeit metaphorically. This strategy starts by helping you to consider three things: the ghosts embedded in your past stories, your present and the potential in your future.

I quickly learned that you could teach a young adult to read if you helped them to believe in themselves, but more importantly, if you made sure that the books recommended were relevant or interesting to them. Without a doubt, I learned that young adults related to the car strategy. Its use of car imagery helped to break down the young men's bravado in a way that made sense to them. I will never forget when one young man showed me the draft of a small book he'd written about his life. It moved me to tears.

Books have the power to take people to new worlds, and not everyone in prison is able to read. Many don't see or believe in their own potential. Fortunately, despite many prisons being far from what they could be, some great work does go on. More employers around the country are seeing the potential in recruiting people from prison. Several of the high street chains and global brands you might shop in, from Timpson to Iceland, Tesco to DHL and Greggs, have robustly embraced this. But it's not just big names; even some forward-thinking smaller employers are seeing this potential, like the indie bookshop chain Bookish, who even donated books to prisons as well as employed people behind bars. All are finding the recruitment of ex-prisoners incredibly rewarding to their existing workforce and, importantly, it is a smart business strategy. The hidden potential and talent festering behind bars is breathtaking and should never be underestimated by any emotionally intelligent HR department.

We should never judge a book by its cover. One of the young men loved David Attenborough and nature books. He suffered from acute ADHD and focus issues, and his childhood had been like a horror film for both him and his brother. I managed to locate him a copy of *Blue Planet*, and later learned when unpicking his story that a teacher had calmed him down as a child using videos of David Attenborough. Much like in *A Christmas Carol*, when you look at the metaphorical ghosts in your life, you will find reason and understanding, but what you do with that discovery moving forward is the key.

Every one of the young men and front-line staff are in my thoughts and prayers. The experience during lockdown was Heaven and Hell all rolled into one, and often man-made – but despite ending up with PTSD, the experience of having to step-up and be a metaphorical father-figure to so many broken young men taught me more than anything in my life.

Only last week I saw one of the young men and was given a fist bump out of respect – young adults rarely do handshakes! – and his first words were 'I'm still reading', and the next were 'is your book out yet?' I was able to show him the book cover and was humbled when I saw him almost moved to tears at the illustration of a father holding a child.

I've said it earlier but it's so important that I am going to say it again; never judge a book by its cover – so many broken young adults have more humanity and potential than anyone gives them credit for. Yes, they needed boundaries and guidance, and some could be very dangerous – but so few of them had good childhoods and never really stood a chance, and if you still don't get it, read or watch Charles Dickens' *Oliver Twist* again, because few things I've seen capture the realities of how young men so often get lost in a cycle of crime. They might eventually become criminals, but so many are victims first. Life and what you're born into isn't always just, and the pages behind all of our stories are often more complex than the external covers and labels suggest.

IF YOU'RE NOT FIGHTING OUT OF LOVE, YOU NEVER REALLY WIN

You only have to look at the news to consider the profound truth in this statement, and I often used it with young men in prison to underpin why violence wasn't worth it. As I complete the final chapters of this book, children and parents are being blown apart around the world – often in fights that have absolutely nothing to do with them – dying as someone somewhere decides to dish out their own versions of hell, often in the name of a false justice.

Life is not always easy and we all must have a fighting spirit in order to survive. Trust me, writing this book nearly broke me at times because it caused so many memories to resurface, and I know that when I finally publish it, I will be judged until the end of time. But I'm writing this out of love, so fighting to finish and publish it has a profound meaning, and a meaning that goes beyond the self.

I've often considered what the word 'love' really means. It's used so easily and often without much thought. To me, love starts and ends by going beyond the self. You feel a deep emotion for something or someone, and it's more important than you or your ego. I believe that when you allow this to happen, you then become one – if only in mind and spirit – with what you're focusing on. So, by this simple definition, if you're not fighting out of love, you're fighting out of pain, and this pain feeds the demons inside and creates separation.

The whole point of Christian religion is to bring us back from our separation to God. Whether you believe in God or not, trust me, when you love and surrender yourself and your ego, you reach a state of peace or Heaven. When you fight, hate or lead with anger or judgement, you become separated and create a form of Hell.

I will never forget sitting in an office talking, oddly enough, to a wing manager about a book for one of the young men who wanted to read about character and boxing. When alarm bells rang, everyone ran. It turns out that two of the young men had had a fight and did some considerable damage to each other. The fight was over paint for their cell walls, mostly driven by ego and control.

One of the men had lost their grandmother a few weeks earlier and couldn't go to the funeral, so I found a cross for him to wear in memory of the woman who had helped to bring him up. During the fight, the cross got broken, with one man holding the chain and the other holding the cross. This upset them more than the original fight or any physical injuries sustained during. When separated and back behind their cell doors, all they cared about was how to fix the cross and whether the other person was okay. I hasten to add, they didn't get the Conor McGregor book on boxing, but we did find a way to fix the cross. Ego and separation created that fight, and surrendering ego brought consideration, peace and goodwill to both men. I genuinely hate violence, but any fight that's not rooted in love will result in a loss, if only the loss of your sanity and humanity for a moment in time.

CULTURE EATS POLICY FOR BREAKFAST

I first came across this quote when I was on a leadership programme in 2012. One of the most impressive leaders I ever met was a Vice President of Swisscom. I sadly don't remember her background completely, but she was something close to an astrophysicist before joining Swisscom. At Swisscom, she was charged with helping to change the mindset of a global corporation facing innovation, attempting to move away from being a typical telecoms provider to a trusted adviser on communications in an evolving marketplace. Over the last few decades, I've heard many leaders speak and have met a fair few after they've spoken. I can genuinely say nobody has ever impressed me as much.

She spent some time helping me create a document focusing on rehabilitation and encouraged me to use the quote 'culture eats policy for breakfast' as a bench line. You only need to consider government policy and how it's often implemented. Policymakers must never forget that the culture which implements that policy will define the way it's delivered. This applies in school, prisons, in a church and with church leaders – you only have to consider safeguarding to understand this, and it certainly applies at home with parenting and families. Policy is often rooted with a mission statement and an agenda, but culture is rooted in humanity, leadership and all the complexities they both bring.

The old saying 'you can bring a horse to water but not make it drink' underpins this issue far better than I can. Any leader who really understands culture change knows that it's all about taking people on a journey with you and setting boundaries and belief in the policy. Without it, you have nothing. Culture change is possible, but it takes time, or runs the risk of being a bumpy start to be resisted by all. Humanity doesn't always like change or rules – and so often policy is made by people who are so far disconnected with the culture they are trying to influence, their attempts are about as much use as a chocolate tea pot. Not to mention, policymakers and leaders come and go, but each create their own twists and turns which front-line staff and managers then have to try and make sense of as they steer their ships. As soon as a front line manager gets the policy in place, another leader comes and changes everything with their own rebooted policy.

Inspiring genuine culture change works in the same way as inspiring a change in children's behaviour. You set clear boundaries and inspire with a loving hand, giving a child a stake in the process of change – whilst making sure the stake or change makes sense to them – repeating the process until it is firmly rooted into their thoughts, feelings and behaviours. A loving brainwash, if you will.

Policy is so often used to make grand statements and cover the cracks. You only have to look at leaders during lockdown to consider their culture tragically allowed them to eat their own policies for breakfast all too often. Do as I say not as I do. But when people are led with integrity and belief in policy, making people part of the desired culture change *can* work, if given time. We have evidence of this with smoking. The other area to consider with culture change is that it may have unintended consequences as people seek alternatives. So many people applauded the changes in smoking, but few considered the long-terms risks of vaping – especially for children – and we have yet to find out just how damaging this new behaviour is. Policy and culture change can often have unintended consequences, which is why any policy makers really do need to think about the culture around what the policy is for. For smokers, this was a culture of social addiction, a behaviour now shifted onto vaping habits.

Another example of this is the way that so many people have been encouraged to speak out about mental health, which is great. But the waiting lists for counselling or trauma therapy often run into years because of a lack of support from the government. Getting our heads together around mental health and minds at work is incredibly important, as is taking the time to ask for help and listen, but embedding the support needed to feed the culture change is equally as important, or you run the risk of setting people up to fail – and simply having a cool policy slogan. So many leaders and celebrities who encourage us to do something don't come close enough to living in the real world to understand how the infrastructure or culture really work in practice, an infrastructure which is severely lacking at present.

WHEN THEY GO LOW, YOU GO HIGH

It is inevitable that one day someone will do or say something that impacts your life. We can either respond with force, or we can rise above it like an eagle on headwinds. There's no question that the high road is not always the easiest path to take. Sometimes this route is not always paved with forgiveness, but rather an understanding that you're better – or at least your thoughts, words and actions are better – than the people who have taken you to a low point in your life. Nelson Mandela is a leader who exemplified this attitude better than most, as did Gandhi. Mandela used the profound humility acquired whilst unjustly serving time to go on and inspire a nation and generations following his release from prison. Gandhi also used the power of will without violent force to help his people.

We heard it from Jesus; he prayed to his Father in Heaven and said, 'Forgive them, for they know not what they have done.' Whilst it's not always easy, taking the high ground will provide you the freedom and space to move on. This high ground is where the peace that passes all understanding resides. Another nugget of wisdom I learnt from Dr Wayne Dyer is that you can often choose to be happy or right, but not always both. Knowing what to stand up and fight for versus what to let go of is often rooted in humility and wisdom.

Years ago, I recall a project imploding after a commercial dispute when an organisation u-turned on an agreement that saw some very good people impacted as a result. I first met this organisation's leadership team after winning two awards for a new business I started, and I even changed the direction of my business for them at great cost to myself. I had to watch as they steadily and repeatedly moved the goal posts to a point that left the integrity of my own work unsustainable.

After a time, I brought in commercial lawyers and my local MP, and everyone fought for justice; it became like a crusade. I was a dog with a bone and my anger became a spare part of me. My team and I had been impacted by poor leadership of others – people who had their own agenda and much larger pockets than us – but for a long time I couldn't move on, blinded by rage and injustice.

Many years later, I would come to realise that the time lost and the emotional and financial impact of fighting a battle bigger than I could afford simply wasn't worth it. This organisation wasn't worth it. I truly believe that nothing is wasted in life, and in some ways the experience of that time and journey have given me a newfound wisdom and helped me to help others. But for a few short years, I flew into a storm of self-righteous indignation. I know I was right to stand up and fight for the people I loved, to a point, but allowing that fight to become a crusade achieved nothing. I collided with the headwinds. Had I used that energy to soar above the storm and create something new, my life would have been so much easier, and a great deal of pain might have been prevented.

The old saying 'you can win the battle but not the war' is profound. I now always consider if any journey, battle or experience is going to allow my soul to soar like an eagle, or plunge to the ground hobbling around like a bird with a broken wing. As the saying goes: 'not forgiving someone is like drinking poison and expecting the other person to die'.

It is easy to fall into the trap of sharing our stories over and over until they become a caricature of who we really are. I learned while working with the young adults that my wisdom was bestowed upon me through my life story, but I certainly wasn't the story or labels I or others gave myself, and never would be.

I believe in the power of memoir, autobiography and testimony when it's written with love and not to make a point or for an agenda. Partly because, as Prince Harry likely learned with his biography *Spare*, people will take your life out of context; they will sensationalise the parts they want, and other people are always impacted by the consequences of the narrative. In reading *Spare,* I certainly recognised some of the similarities around Harry's early years with some of the young men I mentored battling addiction, broken families and emotional demons beyond their control, searching for justice in an unjust world. Perhaps what is worst of all is that people don't always care enough to handle your most cherished thoughts and feelings, and may never understand your truth because they cannot walk in your shoes.

I firmly believe if you are ever able to publish anything, it has to be grounded in love or you run the risk of being part of the problem and not the solution, and you will encounter considerable headwinds.

Prince Harry was brave enough to combat the injustices done to him in court, recently winning a case against invasive media. However, unlike so many, Harry has access to resources which many of us do not. While David and Goliath is a great story, the reality is that without considerable resources to hold power to account, especially in commercial law, this sort of result is almost impossible. This is why documenting history is so important. One benefit of our developing society and technology is that is even mere mortals have the power to document and publish (and build a platform beyond the mainstream media) these days, which does enhance an individual sense of social justice.

One of the most grounding parts of bookselling is realising that most books – even bestsellers – have a shelf life, and will one day end up in the bargain bin or charity shop. As every publisher and good bookstore knows, having too many spare copies of a title is never a good thing. As I worked my Christmas shifts stocking shelves, I remember hearing George Michaels song *Last Christmas* rise to number one and couldn't help reflecting on the irony of the lyrics as I was shelved books about the late Queen. Bestsellers last Christmas, yet hardly glanced at this year. Time changes everything and nothing lasts forever. Even books have the same reality of succession, unless they become classics or find a new readership.

NO STORM LASTS FOREVER

Wayne Dyer first introduced me to the idea that no storm lasts forever, a concept which I used over and over, especially when the world shut down during the pandemic. I'm sure you've already realised but there are sayings and quotes scattered throughout this book, and many of them used to belong to a wall calendar which I created for myself in 2020, called my 'God 4 Sake' calendar.

One of the young adults I worked with was a talented artist, and very kindly created me a piece of artwork with all the quotes on as a thank you gift. He placed the words I'd repeated to him the most – No Storm Lasts Forever – at the centre of the artwork.

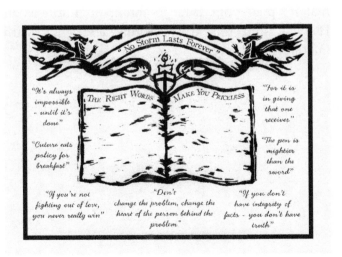

And whilst I don't know much or have all the answers, Wayne Dyer was right. No storm will last forever; we all come into the world with nothing but our spirit and leave with nothing but our spirit. During our own journeys, we will all encounter storm clouds and rainbows. The reality is that we are hopefully on a journey towards eternal life and peace; even if we are not, every storm we encounter on Earth will reach its end at some point.

This is why we pray that people may rest in peace after they pass away. The key is not getting to the end of your life wondering whether you got it wrong somewhere along the way. Sure, we will all get things wrong at times – I certainly know I have, and I deeply regret that with my heart and soul – but until we take our last breath, it's never too late to have one moment in time when you can match up to your true potential, on Earth as in Heaven, and this truly begins and ends with unconditional love.

WHERE THERE IS HATRED, LET ME BRING LOVE

As I've repeatedly explained throughout this book, the man who helped me through most of my storms was Dr Wayne Dyer – combined with my profound faith in God, of course.

Wayne taught me to use the following prayer to guide me on my way. I have a version of it on my desk and always near me, and I try to say it every time I wake or go to sleep. This prayer is the cornerstone of this book and everything that is to come in my life, until I take my last breath on Earth. I hope it brings you as much solace as it gives me.

A prayer of St Francis of Assisi:

Lord, make me an instrument of your peace; where there is hatred, let me sow love; where there is injury, pardon; where there is discord, union; where there is doubt, faith; where there is despair, hope; where there is darkness, light; and where there is sadness, joy.

O Divine Master, grant that I may not so much seek to be consoled as to console; to be understood, as to understand; to be loved, as to love; for it is in giving that we receive, it is in pardoning that we are pardoned, and it is in dying that we are born to eternal life. Amen.

BREAKING BREAD

My father was one of the hardest workers I ever knew. He had several businesses; a post office, florists, green grocers to bakeries, to sandwich and coffee shops. He loved the sun and was an avid exerciser. He especially loved to cycle, row and run marathons. Whatever he did he excelled at, each hobby was well researched. Above it all, my father was intensely kind. He had his own childhood demons from when his own father was away at war, and I often suspect that he was a sensitive soul as a child. When I was a child observing him, I noticed that he always seemed to be in competition with life itself – I think that trait resides in most exceptional entrepreneurs. He would do anything for anyone and had a heart of gold, but business did come before family. At times, he felt like a father not a dad, often missing in action for business reasons. My father did have an addictive personality, whether this was in work or play, and certainly struggled with alcohol towards the end of his life.

When I was a child, he became a master baker and went on to run an award-winning bakery and later an incredible coffee shop, way before coffee shops became a thing. He was sweet enough to name his bakeries after my mother, putting her name up in lights. His battles with alcohol started to get out of hand when his flagship business was compulsorily purchased to make way for a new shopping centre. The stress of this, amongst a few other things, took him down a path he never fully recovered from. I still see two of his last businesses with queues out the door and I'm reminded of his

130

hard work, entrepreneurial spirit and love of business. That said, I also see the space where his flagship business used to stand mostly empty because the new shopping centre they built never took off. So, in the end, it was all a futile waste by a property developer who didn't care about my father.

So often in life, situations come and impact our lives, and the titans of business or government bulldoze their ways through the hopes and dreams of anyone who gets in their way. Just look at the political land grab for the now derailed HS2 high speed rail track.

Dad's kindness and baking businesses never fail to remind me of the power in breaking bread together. Often during Christian mass, we are given bread or a communion wafer to signify the receiving of the body of Christ. During the last supper, Christ told the disciples he was going to be betrayed and killed. He broke bread to signify his body and poured wine to represent his blood. Christians are urged to carry out this practice in remembrance of how Christ gave his life to save them and give them eternal life with our Father in Heaven.

It is inevitable that there will be situations in our life that are beyond our control; people will betray us. Whilst the impact of these situations might last a lifetime, I've come to realise that there is a way to weather the storms. We can lean on a faith larger than ourselves and walk away from the darkness that might engulf us by focusing on the light. I can't smell freshly baked bread without thinking of my father and my childhood, or walk past one of his old shops without remembering his love of business and tireless hard work. Because of addictions on both sides while I was growing up, life wasn't always easy for us, but there was no question that I loved my father regardless. So many of the things I am most proud of came to me through him, including my desire to help others, but a few of life's battles also hinged from trying to navigate his demons and my own.

Breaking bread together is one of the greatest ways to nurture new friendships and sustain old ones, but I've never forgotten that a great baker puts their heart and soul into the process and uses the very best of ingredients nature has to provide – giving it time to rise in a warm stable environment, trusting that the yeast will work in time. Likewise, when we do the same in life, the outcome is astonishing, but we so often don't look after our minds, bodies or families, and instead focus on the wrong things until it's too late. One thing is for sure: even when the storm passes, and we lose somebody, the love for them rarely passes. If we are honest with ourselves, and over time, with reflection, understanding and forgiveness, peace replaces the pain.

I think that was why Wayne Dyer talked about forgiveness being his greatest teacher when he stood by his father's grave. Whatever our journeys in life, most of us can only do our best. Sometimes that falls short of what we might wish for ourselves, each other or our parents, but it doesn't have to diminish the love within our hearts and minds. This is what will last for an eternity, if we let go of the sorrow, walk out of the darkness and into the light of forgiveness.

I WILL ALWAYS LOVE YOU

By now you will understand the love I have for books, lyrics, words and music, not to mention people. It hasn't always been – and isn't always – that way, which is why I need to frequently read the prayer of St Francis. Like everyone on Earth, I'm a work in progress.

There is an icebreaker I've encountered several times in life: if you could have a dinner party or meet someone, who you would want it to be? My answer is always without a doubt Dolly Parton. I think her humanity, self-belief, emotional intelligence, talent, heart and legacy are astonishing, and I truly admire her.

I love the fact that she took the power and joy of a rag coat and turned it into a coat of many colours. She turned a life of extreme poverty into a one of abundance, giving and wonder. Her love of children and books empowered her to create an imagination library that reaches millions of children around the world. And trust me, giving children the power to read, and a love of reading, is one of the greatest gifts you can ever give.

Everyone knows Whitney Houston's classic ballad, 'I Will Always Love You', but not everyone knows that it was originally written by Dolly Parton or why. She was in an abusive and controlling relationship, and when she finally decided to step away, she left with nothing – he kept the lot. So, she wrote the song to him. She used words to make her point and to set both parties free. The benefit of that was she reaped a much greater reward. She left with nothing, but still managed to use a foundation of unconditional love to transmute the injustice into something that pays her considerable dividends to this day. And further, those dividends and resources are used to help friends, family and people around the world, bringing comfort and joy to many lives.

Dolly mentors many fledgling artists and knows how to be a shining star and servant leader. Sure, she used her image to make fun of herself and the world around her, learning the power of not taking herself too seriously. However, because she knew who she was, the labels didn't stick; her talent speaks for itself, and her heart creates more good than the average humans does. Dolly went from a coat of rags to a coat of many colours, from working nine to five to owning DOLLYWOOD, a musical fairground and beyond. Now, she is a lady of faith and conviction, and certainly knows her Father in Heaven and on Earth.

Her power came by knowing to lead and leave with love in your heart – and your voice. She knew that children and the world will listen if you have the courage to say the right words.

FOR IT IS IN GIVING THAT ONE RECEIVES

'For it is in giving that one receives'. Anyone who gives unconditionally knows the profound truth in this message. Giving not to receive is at the heart of unconditional love.

I think my kindness and desire to give came from my parents, but I learned the transformational power of giving during lockdown. While working with the young adults, it crossed my mind that many of them thought they didn't matter and that nobody cared, especially on their birthdays. Many had self-worth issues that were rooted in the chaos of their births and early years. Some had families that cared but couldn't be there for them, and some had parents missing in action.

So, after realising many would become reflective or withdrawn around their birthdays, especially when the world was in lockdown, I decided to make a small token birthday pack and get a card signed by everyone, or at least as many people as possible, grudges and turf wars permitting. I had a meeting with the prison director who loved the idea and realised it could be used, in part, to rehabilitate and mitigate the lack of visitation and isolation which the young people were forced to experience, often thinking that nobody cared about them – which was far from the truth.

136

This small initiative created a new culture on the wing; it cheered people up and it honoured that someone believed they had value. Don't get me wrong, it wasn't all sunshine and rainbows – far from it, in fact – but if a young adult read their first book, had a birthday, or managed to read several books, we would honour it with a small gift or prize. I saw this rewards incentive in turn create a situation where they started to consider other people. In their own small way, the young adults started learning how to care about themselves and the world around them. Which, trust me, is key to rehabilitation.

Over time, the wing went from one of the most challenging to one where staff wanted to work, and young people steadily felt safer. Sure, it wasn't always a breeze, but in the early days the wing was like a war zone, and that's not something I say lightly. Many things beyond the reward scheme occurred to create that change, including new professional pro-social staff who listened and cared, bringing on older people to mentor the youngsters. In a way, even the natural boundaries caused by the pandemic created less intensity with landings being split at recreation. But most important of all was that by having a manager who cared – and the lady in charge of the young adult wing certainly did care – we collectively managed to fight against the tide. This was hugely important for all, because only months before I arrived, a young man sadly took his own life. The operational manager and I were determined not to let this happen again, especially during the increased pressures of lockdown.

You see, suicide prevention, especially in prisons, is close to my heart. In fact, one of my friends, who sadly passed away from cancer, was a former probation officer and Samaritan who created the Samaritans prison listener's scheme. Her work started over thirty years ago and she went on to become the Vice President of the Samaritans. She developed the power of peer mentorship and went on to help many countries around the world, including Africa, to set up mentoring and suicide prevention schemes.

My friend believed in the power of listening and kindness, and when she was in the last stages of cancer, she wanted to see *Paddington II*. The only problem was that it was only showing in the cinema, and she was too ill to go. A friend of mine from one of my leadership programmes managed to get her a copy via their friends at BAFTA. Like the late Queen, Kathy loved Paddington. *Paddington II* also shows how bringing light into the soul of a prison can create a culture change. Paddington is rooted in kindness, and my friend was too.

She wanted to get a thank you gift for the man who secured the DVD. I found a lovely book for them called *The Little Book of Kindness*, and when we opened its cover, we both smiled upon seeing that the book cited learning to listen as one of the greatest forms of kindness a person can bestow.

PATHWAYS, SNAKES AND LADDERS

One of my favourite songs was called 'Pathways', written by a breakout artist called Billy Lockett. I'm not sure what happened to the song in the end as it seems to have disappeared from the internet, but for a while it was charted in the BBC. Its lyrics underpinned that in the past it used to be about the music, and now it was often about the men in suits deciding your fate. It's certainly true that the music industry has evolved and changed, and not everyone finds justice in how they are paid or how their work is valued; this is especially a problem with modern streaming platforms.

It's certainly easier now than it ever was for any artist to create a starting platform and get their message out there, but we do live in a world that commercialises everything, and that then gets to define what's made, released or how it's valued. So many artists lose control of their lives and work, and much as George Michael found when taking on the might of Sony, it's hard to protect your rights from the men in suits who decide your fate.

So many people put you on a 'Pathway' selling you a dream which you think will set you free, but these paths can also be like snakes and ladders. Teaching our children to understand this in a world that's so often unjust and weighted against the little guy is so important.

Streaming giants and artists are still struggling to get the balance right. But one lesson I've learned when starting out or being sold a dream is that all that glistens isn't gold. In life, we will always encounter people who wish to decide our fate; they can act for the greater good or they can act for themselves, and discerning which is which might be the difference between success, peace and joy, or failure. My continual advice is to never judge a book by its cover; this applies to a lawyer by their contracts, or an offer that seems too good to be true. Like in the new *Wonka* film, there is importance in the fine print. Not everyone can have the knack of bypassing snakes and climbing the ladder, whilst also finding a way to reclaim their own work, like Taylor Swift has. Some people are left tangled in the wake of other people's pathways, unsure of exactly who is deciding their fate.

LONDON BRIDGE IS FALLING DOWN

About a year ago, I noticed on my way into work that a car windscreen had been smashed in, leaving a considerable amount of glass on the pavement. For whatever reason, nobody decided to ever clean it up, leaving it to the winds of time to blow the shards away. The problem was that this glass was working itself into passersby shoe soles. I remember more than once discovering glass shards trodden into my home. Even a year on, despite countless storms, a small bit of glass remains on the side of that busy road. This is a good metaphor for pain in our hearts and souls; memories and experiences can bring with them shards of glass into our spirits. To underpin this, I used to host an event for employers in which I would hold up a jar of coffee. The jar looked okay and intact; nobody would have thought anything was wrong. But the jar was in fact broken and shards of glass had fallen into the coffee. Only the outer mask of plastic and brand image kept you from realising that what was inside might be damaged or dangerous if you were to consume it. Like the lesson of not judging a book by its cover, this was an exceptional metaphor for life.

For anyone who ever reads this book and thinks it may just be focused on wanting to help the people who find themselves in prison, whether that is a physical or emotional prison, I want to stop you in your tracks. My point when fighting for justice of a prisoner or ex-prisoner is that if you don't heal the hurt, you run the risk of doing more harm in the long run; this applies to emotional imprisonment, too. Rehabilitation only works when it's delivered well; when we strip rehabilitation to its very core, it's actually about little more than repairing the soul. This was a message that we learned when looking at the three crosses and contemplating justice on Good Friday nearly two thousand years ago. Even if you don't believe in God, you must consider that all rehabilitation, spiritual or otherwise, starts with the person in the mirror. Acceptance of oneself and one's actions is the cornerstone of genuine rehabilitation.

The only problem with this is that, as anyone who has ever worked around the criminal justice sector will know, words mean very little; it's the substance of the words that matter – the character and actions behind the person or words. So often people will say what they think someone else *wants* them to hear. A reporter once asked why anyone would want to work in prison or probation, but if you strip the job to its very core, it's about helping to save souls, and what could be more just or rewarding?

The problem is that, if the basics aren't done properly in childhood, behind bars or beyond, work on rehabilitation can all come tumbling down. I remember considering this after a PC Keith Palmer bravely lost his life whilst standing guard outside the Palace of Westminster during the 2017 terrorist attack. And then again, when two Cambridge graduates lost their lives on London Bridge whilst helping to run a rehabilitation event for Learning Together. I actually knew Jack personally; Jack Merritt and Saskia Jones were incredible human beings, working to transform lives, and tragically lost their young lives at the hands of a man they wanted to help.

That said, other offenders ran to help and put their lives at risk in the process. The point I am making here is that nothing is black and white when considering the humanity of someone going through rehabilitation. However – and this is a big however – the experience and journey of supporting and evaluating the person is essential. Whilst the saying 'fake it, till you make it' might be something promoted on a leadership course or within a self-help book, the reality is often faking it and *not* making it. People can hide who they are for a time, but when squeezed, the truth will come out, just like with Dr Wayne Dyer's orange. This is why any safeguarding – be it in a church, prison or hospital, even government – must be the responsibility of all and never just one person. If something is missed and not brought to swift attention, this can ultimately lead to loss of life, at the hands of oneself or another.

People will always slip through the cracks, but in my experience whenever we look back on a tragedy – especially around terrorism – there were signs that were noticed but not voiced. Someone saw a sign, and more often than not didn't have the courage to speak up; or worse, when they did, nobody cared to listen or do anything about it. Speaking up and listening is sometimes the bravest and most valuable skill we can teach our kids. Trust me, communication with support and integrity, regardless of who you are, is key. When things go wrong, as they tragically often do, normally more than one person's failing has allowed it to get to that point. We are in this journey together, from the cradle to the grave, and we forget that at our peril.

WHISTLE DOWN THE WIND

In life, and especially behind bars, people are told to keep their mouths shut or simply look the other way. You only have to consider the injustices done to man and children at the hands of churches and clergy across the world to consider this point.

I learned first-hand that blowing the whistle isn't easy; it's always a judgement call. I remember considering the situation for months before I spoke out, knowing that doing the morally right thing might cause a pushback and would certainly lose me friends at the risk of influencing nothing. That said, in my case, after months of soul searching, I felt I had to speak out about what was wrong. When I did, the first thing that I had to justify was why I had spoken up, what I wanted to come from it and what my motives were. I was then analysed by a group of people, my motives put to trial.

In the eye of any storm, speaking up and standing firm in your truth will ultimately reach somebody. It might not be in the way you want, or during the timeline you anticipated, and you will rarely find the justice you originally set out to gain. But like oil and water, truth will rise to the surface given time.

Humanity frequently chooses not to respect or honour whistle-blowing, choosing to instead demonise it. What I've learned most in life is that evil really does flourish when good people do nothing. Plausible deniability is used far too much in this world. If society is to change, and it must if we are meant to survive, we have to find better ways of listening and supporting someone when they speak up and blow the whistle. We must start to cherish truth, rather than fearing it, looking the other way, or shutting it down. Integrity isn't always present from birth and it certainly isn't present in all leaders. Character, attitude and responsibility can be taught, but only when rooted in respect.

In my whistle-blowing experience, many people chose to either not look or care. Many would give up as their pleas fell on deaf ears, but this only pushed me harder. While I wish I could turn back time on many of my life experiences, blowing the whistle isn't one of them. The one time I firmly blew the whistle was worth the storm that came my way, even though it lasted for more years than it should. It was worth it, not because of the outcome, but because the experience played a significant part in helping me to build character, attitude and respect. Over a decade later, one of the first people to look at the situation is now a firm friend, a friendship is rooted in mutual respect and understanding. Neither of us were able to get the justice the situation deserved, but character building doesn't come without cost – another point our Father in Heaven tried to teach some two thousand years ago.

We can either be a good Samaritan or simply walk by and pretend not to notice. The choice is ours to make; after all, we have free will, or at least an illusion of it. Unfortunately, due to various inequalities and injustices, not everyone has a voice. Most people who have changed the world or its history have done so by believing in the power of speaking up. Even if they lost their life in the process, I have no doubt they found their true soul, while those who remained silent lost a small part of theirs.

DON'T DIE WITH YOUR MUSIC STILL IN YOU

Another quote I learnt from the late great Dr Wayne Dyer is 'don't die with your music still in you.' It's also a quote I used with the young adults to underpin that they must not waste their dreams, potential and talents.

Wayne Dyer had eight children, and I remember that when I stepped away from my leadership fellow role at St George's House, his oldest daughter said that Wayne would have been proud of me for going my own way. He did something similar when he gave up being a professor of psychology and a secure job and tenure for life to write his first book, *Your Erroneous Zones*, which has sold over 60 million copies to date. Sometimes you have to follow your instincts and let go of something solid, or something that doesn't feel right for you, to actually grow and make room for the art, book or song within, whatever that may be. His oldest daughter did that herself when she gave up a great job to start her own company.

One of Wayne's other daughters wrote a lovely book, actually titled *Don't Die With Your Music Still in You*, alongside him. They knew that we are all creative beings. They certainly understood the pain caused to a human soul by holding ones creative force inside, let alone getting to the end of your life and realising you may have wasted your time on Earth by not doing what you loved or wanted to. We are all born with the potential to create havoc or create good, but so much of our time alive seems to be defined by the good opinions of others, or rooted in their fears and limiting dreams. It takes courage to walk the road less travelled, or to at least try, but our time on Earth is so brief, no one should keep their potential locked inside.

Imagine the tragedy of the invention, artwork, book, business, journey or award that's never reached its creation. Teaching a child not to die with their music still in them is one of the greatest lessons of all. It's how you live a self-fulfilling and self-actualised life. If you're not living your own life, you're living someone else's, and there is absolutely no justice in that.

SAINT GEORGE SLAYED THE DRAGON

We all have real or emotional dragons to slay. If we don't find a way, they can consume us, drain our energy, or at worst take our lives. Many countries and rulers have chosen St George as their patron saint, allowing the legends and myths to empower and embolden an image of strength which they believe transcends all. The elusive St George did actually exist, but when all is said and done – like so many legends and people with labels, titles and iconic images before them – he was simply a human being behind a shield. This isn't to say that legends haven't done great things, but they can often fall short of reality. The old adage 'be careful if you meet your hero – because they might not be what you expect' is all too often the case. Trust me, I know. If we don't find ways to lovingly slay the dragons or demons before us, they will destroy our best parts. So often, we need to believe in something greater than ourselves to achieve this; as Christians, we believe that if we can't get justice, we can pray and believe our Father in Heaven can.

Leaders have carefully selected St George throughout time as a force for justice, strength, bravery and power. Good versus evil, and yet only unconditional love can ever really slay any emotional dragon or imbue us with the strength to let go.

As parents and mentors, we try to give our children metaphorical shields to protect them in life, but even we know that if they try to slay their dragons with force, that force is likely to overwhelm and hurt them in return. After all, yes, hitting out in self-defence is a defence, but it's not a very good one, just a reason. This brings us back to the idea that by taking an eye for an eye, we run the risk of blinding a nation. You only have to turn on the news tonight or pick up a newspaper to see the divine truth within this statement. Action poisoned in anger only ever results in more pain. Loving defence brings protection and healing. One person's justice is often another person's injustice – and the cycle of damage, death and destruction keep growing. Like it or not, we do reap what we sow.

Finding ways to help children create their own shields and how to slay the anger, jealousy and resentment that might boil up from time to time is of great importance. Helping them to look beyond the myths, icons and legends that leaders and celebrities so often create for an illusion of power and justice is equally important.

Legend had it that St George slayed a dragon – but did he really? Have we ever had dragons that breathe fire, or saints who slayed anything other than the darkness within before the darkness around them? Any good news, even the Bible, is taken at face value and should be appraised with considered thought. Not everything spoken around religion is true – sometimes the metaphors, translations, myths and legends are distorted by man's interpretation of them. This is why there are so many facets to religion, after all. We all have a responsibility to help children to decipher what is true and what is not.

BRING HIM HOME

I don't know if you have ever heard the song 'Bring Him Home'. In it, we hear someone beseech God to protect a soldier and bring him home from war. The person notes that the soldier is like a son to him, and even does what so many of us try to do with God: barter for the outcome we want. In this song, the man is offering up himself in sacrifice.

War is never a good thing, and yet it is a trap which we have fallen into since the beginning of time. You'd hope humanity would learn from the past, but we rarely do. As I look around the world at the moment, we are lying when we say we are not at war. History has often been the toughest critic of the reason and justice for ever going to war, but it's hard. We do need to defend ourselves, and the men and women who put their lives on the line for us and fought for our freedom are absolute heroes. I used to work and live next door to a former marine and would often go for walks with him. Whenever I did, I noticed our pace expanded my normal ability and his strength took me beyond my own. He so often questioned the point of some of the wars and situations he'd found himself in, and I will never forget the look in his eyes on Remembrance Day. Love, pain, honour and respect – and above all else, strength and humility.

One day I hope humanity will only recall war as a footnote in history, but I can't see how that will ever be possible when leaders routed in ego run the world. If ever you want proof evil exists, just look to what man is capable of doing in the name of war and remember that's also embedded in the word 'justice'. Maybe now you see we can never get absolute justice – certainly not when evil exists. Unless there's a miracle, man's inhumanity upon itself will grow until society as it is self-destructs.

I don't pray 'bring him home' – I pray bring them all home. Never forget that during World War One, enemies did pause on Christmas Day 1914. The day our savour was born. Then ego set in, and they started to kill each other again; we lost sight of humanity. The key to peace is igniting and sustaining that moment of pure humanity and respect for our fellow man and trying to prevent evil from getting a foothold into leadership, and the hearts and minds of our fellow man in the first place. Dictators do not suddenly appear. We permit them. A reminder: 'the only thing necessary for triumph of evil is that good men do nothing'.

SILENT NIGHT

When I was in the eye of a storm, I nearly went to live in a Church of England convent. Yes, picture *Sister Act*; it wasn't that different. I never forgot them asking if I would mind that at times it was a silent order. I replied that I feel most a peace in silence, and it's true. I've always been a little reclusive since I was a child, and I'm certainly at peace with being alone.

I am a firm believer that the saying 'silence is golden' is true.

One of the things the convent sisters would say was 'You know we weren't always sisters – we had normal lives before we dedicated our lives to God'. It didn't take long to understand the humanity behind the habit and that they had their own ego battles just as we do – much the same for any cleric, priest or bishop. Religion and faith are different. One is man-made and one is not. They often run parallel, but faith is a personal experience, and nobody can ever walk in another's shoes or experience faith in the same way. That said, we can come together in prayer, remembrance and celebration of being one with our Father in Heaven. I believe silence is where peace resides, and I don't just mean noise. If you want to discover a Holy night, pray for a silent one first. I do believe that God speaks to and through us all – but his voice is so gentle and his touch so light, we frequently miss it.

Teaching a child to value peace is where mindfulness resides, and thankfully, spiritual or not, the world is slowly waking to the concept of mindfulness and meditation. And we must; the pace of the world and the voice of humanity is getting louder by the day, and that noise is separating us from one another, ourselves and creation.

IT'S ALWAYS IMPOSSIBLE
UNTIL IT'S DONE

A few years back I was entering a storm I genuinely didn't think I would survive, and for one brief moment I contemplated taking my life. This was not my first brush with suicide, but it was my first in well over a decade, and my faith was much stronger than it had been back then. I went on a retreat for a few days, not entirely sure if I'd be back, and one day I found myself on a beach contemplating the storm ahead. I love the poem 'Footprints in the Sand', which asks God if he is there why are there no footsteps, and he pointed out that he was carrying them, so we only see his footprints.

I prayed for about three days. Sadly, there was no sand on my beach, only stones, and then I decided that Wayne Dyer was right, and that everything is always impossible until it's done. I knew the road ahead was going to be dark, but I also knew that no storm lasts forever. I realised if other people were going to go low, I'd have to find a way to go high – but most of all, I wanted to see the journey through. I remembered that I didn't want to die with my music still in me.

I also remembered Jeremiah 29:11 – "'For I know the plans I have for you," declares the Lord, "plans to prosper you and not to harm you, plans to give you hope and a future.'"

I had been squeezed, and I discovered what was inside me. I knew if I was to make it through the storm, I would have to approach it with humility and strength. Which I did, and the results are this book. The fruit of the spirit is helping so many young adults when the world was hit by its greatest storm in modern-day history and finding new friends along the way.

Nothing is ever wasted; if you realise the power of who walks alongside you, mere man is nothing to be afraid of. Just consider; had I not made it through the storm, this illustration wouldn't have been created or used to inspire countless young souls in the eye of their own storm, and one of the world's greatest pandemics.

NO MATTER WHAT THEY TELL YOU

Years ago, I was fortunate enough to know one of the kindest souls to ever walk the Earth, and he was a bloody good singer too. Stephen frequently sung the song 'No Matter What'. The song underpins that children do often know their own minds, something we sometimes forget as we mould them into the beings we want and believe they should be.

I went to Sunday school as a kid and frankly had little interest in or understanding of it. I took religious education classes and didn't learn much. I tried to pray to some bloke I didn't know up in the sky. Then in my thirties, I had a near brush with death, found a faith that's hard to explain and conquered an addiction to prescription medication instantly. Over the years, many friends and I have been hurt by the church, or actions of religious leaders, but nothing has ever made me doubt my faith. Some people have tried to challenge it, and at times I've conceded or hidden it – even been embarrassed by it – but at an intrinsic level, no matter what we are told by others, what we believe at our very core often holds a nugget of truth.

I don't pretend to have all the answers, or understand why so much about faith can seem like a mystical game, but the fact much is that humanity is always searching for answers beyond us; we know a greater force than ourselves must have created us, and the universe around us.

I have friends of all faiths and also of none. One of the men who I most admire is an Iman. He has strength, wisdom and humility pouring from his soul. Many of my Muslim friends have often been more respectful and supportive of my faith than countless Christians I've met along the way, including when I was confirmed by the Archbishop of Canterbury at Easter some years back. By this, I mean insofar as they seemed to understand the profound need to confirm my faith in God within the context of a Christian church, even if our faiths differed in wider context. Now this is something I deeply respected and it greatly touched my heart. I've met archbishops, princes, lords, ladies and politicians in abundance, been in rooms with princesses and leaders of the world, and I've walked with some of society's most broken. But I've only ever met one Christian lady who reminds me of Christ and walks like an angel.

She's called Norma and has a gentle strength that surpasses anything I've ever seen. She never has a bad word to say about anyone. She's supported her church for decades, carefully nurtured children and has the ability to stand with the most broken and not judge, or with the highest of society and not care – she is the closest walking, talking version of Jesus Christ I have ever seen, and being in her presence has taught me what light, unconditional love and friendship really is. I hope one day we all find someone like Norma.

IS THERE A DOCTOR IN THE HOUSE?

When we think about justice in the world, or if God really exists, we often focus on natural disasters, wars, crime or ill health. They all make us wrestle with our creator in heaven – does he exist, how could he let this happen, why does he seem to save one person in a miraculous event, only to ignore the next man, woman or child standing or sadly lying in the street, let alone six feet under?

I have often pondered this line of thought, and even debated the point with my Father in Heaven – albeit in prayer – and I think the answer is paradoxically both so simple and widely complex all at the same time. I go back to a few things I've mentioned before. One is that, if we truly believe in Alpha and Omega, the beginning and the last, God ultimately remains from the beginning to the end of time, and points to eternal life with us. That's not to diminish the pain, hurt, grief and loss that comes when somebody appears to be taken to soon or before their time. When this happens we search for the meaning and justice, or lack thereof, in any given situation. I have learned through grace that it's often during the darkest of times we notice the light. Only under pressure can profound growth and maturity occur.

Behind everything, I truly believe that there is a learning curve which bypasses our understanding at least in this lifetime, maybe when and if we meet our maker and look back beyond the self – it will all make sense. Someone once used the example of a tapestry that when looked at from the back has a chaotic array of threads and knots, but on the other side hold a beautiful image for the world to behold. Maybe just maybe life is like that, and it's not until heaven we can look back on our threads and knots and see the image we so often missed.

I was recently watching an easy-going film called *The Prince and Me* on Amazon Prime and was struck by the words of Prince Edward's father; he essentially said to his family that it's not until the end of your life that you realise the importance of the decisions you make at the beginning.

This sentiment resonated with me last week because I found myself considering my own health and life, and what's to come in the next fifty years… here's hoping! Last week was a little profound for a number of reasons. I found myself consoling two friends who had lost a number of relatives over the Christmas period. One friend's loss included two family members that had reached old age, but also one baby who was just about to be born and never made it beyond her mother's womb, tragically passing in the final month of the pregnancy. As my friend told me of her profound sorrow and grief, I could see her struggling to make sense of the loss. The saying that the eyes are the windows to our soul is beyond true. I remember listening and being drawn to hug my friend as my heart broke for her, but as I walked away in silent prayer, I could not help but ponder on why life has to be so cruel. My only comfort is that hopefully our spirits go on beyond this life, and maybe eternal life and peace do reside with our Father in Heaven. I have no idea why life and death often seem so unjust, like a cruel fateful lottery of chance mixed with grace and a miraculous recovery for the lucky few. To linger on the answer often brings disappointment.

This feeling was also underpinned last week when news broke that the TV presenter Kate Garraway's husband, Derek Draper, tragically passed away in the UK following his battle with the impacts of Long Covid. I heard the news and watched on as social media rose up in profound sorrow – and a touch of judgement (not all humans are kind when looking on at the lives of others). I was only able to send the family a silent prayer.

It is often in one's passing that we remember the times that our lives overlapped. In hearing the news, I couldn't help remembering being lucky enough to be at the launch of one of Derek's businesses at Waterstones Piccadilly, a business that embodied being a leading specialist in psychoanalysis within the corporate sector. At the launch, Kate was proudly by his side, supporting her husband. This of course was to be followed by his book launch for *Create Space* at the institute of directors only a year or so later.

My lasting memory of Derek isn't his political work, his writing, or the impact around his being an exceptional psychoanalyst. Surprisingly, my lasting memory of Derek is the profound love that

163

shone from his family at his book launch. I will never forget his children performing a song on the stage at the launch, amid the political, literacy and media elite. Derek's lasting memory in my eyes was of his children, beaming with pride at being part of their father's special day.

It's interesting looking back on memories in retrospect. On that evening, none of us could have foretold that after leaving an event that sparkled with joy, so much pain and sorrow was to follow the next year thanks to an unknown virus yet to hit our shores. A virus which has taken the lives of so many people before their time, and left us all wondering about the sense of justice in that.

The Covid pandemic made us all face the importance of doctors, nurses and care staff, entrusting our lives to them in an entirely new and unfamiliar way. For a moment in time, the world relied on and clapped for them all. But now, not long after, we watch as so many of those working on the front-line fight for justice around fair pay. And that's not to mention many battling their own legacy of PTSD and exhaustion, following the relentless pandemic which seemed to go on for longer than any of us could have ever anticipated.

No matter who we are, certainly in the Western world, we often begin and end our lives surrounded by the profound gift of doctors and nurses. Without question, when I look around the world, I am mindful that some humans have easier access to medical services than others. I have already mentioned that I have PTSD, but it took a year before I could get counselling, and I was one of the fortunate ones that ended up with an extraordinary counsellor who still supports me to this very day, even as I wrestled with publishing this book or not, knowing I would be judged until the end of time if I did.

I am reminded of my privilege daily; I also require further surgery, but despite it being listed as urgent, the waiting list runs at nearly two years just to see the consultant, unless I can find the funds to go privately; not all of us can do that. That said I am beyond lucky; I have access to one of the best medical practices in the UK, albeit in my humble opinion, and the NHS funding my healthcare – an extraordinary opportunity when you consider other countries and their healthcare systems around the world. Without question, I have been supported with grace, talent and consideration by two exceptional GPs and their support team, especially for the symptoms of my PTSD.

Thank God – or thank Doctors and Nurses – that they go to medical or nursing school for years to help us, and we have selfless projects like Doctors without Borders. It brings me hope in humanity that there are people in this world who choose a vocation which places their life at risk in order to help others, just like all the medical staff did around the world when the pandemic hit. They weren't just in the storm, they were in the eye of it.

But health isn't always respected; the justice on who gets treatment or medication can seem like a cruel and unjust game of chance. Thankfully, we do have people that consider others before themselves, but unfortunately, we sometimes only remember their true value when they are fighting to save our lives or to care for us. Young healthcare professionals are essential to our future and our leaders must nurture and support them appropriately in the UK and beyond. Not all countries have easy access to free medical services, and if the pandemic taught us anything, when the world ground to a halt, beyond the odd prayers and an army of selfless volunteers, it was the doctors, nurses and care staff that became the saints that created the miracles for some of us lucky ones.

The illustration on the cover of this book shows a father holding their child; as the population ages its often the other way round. Life has a cycle to it, and we are all more connected to each other than we might have originally thought. Nobody can get through life on their own, and we should never forget that when a human being enters this world, they are often greeted by a midwife, doctor, or nurse, and when it's time to say goodbye it's often a doctor, nurse or carer standing by the family and bedside as everyone takes their last breath.

Don't ever undervalue anyone working on the front line, because they really do stand with humanity from beginning to the end, albeit if we are lucky enough to live in a part of the world that has access to humanity's most graceful medical professionals. This world often isn't very just, but it certainly could be vastly more so if we all worked together. If you want to understand more about what I mean, I suggest you listen to a song called 'Not Enough' by Dolly Parton. I dare you to listen to it and not agree or at least pause for thought!

I also sometimes wonder that if we are human beings on a spiritual journey, whether we are meant to have justice in the way we think we should. I remember the father of motivation, Dr Wayne Dyer, saying that he genuinely believed he wouldn't have been the man he had become or been able to go on to help millions of people if he hadn't had a deeply flawed father. Wayne believed his father was his greatest teacher. His father had been an alcoholic and had gone to prison, abandoning his wife and children, but Wayne felt his father's mistakes taught him to be self-reliant.

Wayne felt that you couldn't teach self-reliance without being self-reliant first. He certainly felt his father's mistakes taught him to be a better father himself, and undoubtedly taught him the power of forgiveness. Maybe, just maybe, life's injustices are our greatest spiritual teachers and help our souls evolve in ways we don't always understand. I certainly don't have all the answers, but I do know that the situations, mistakes and people that hurt me the most are the people that certainly taught me the most. I don't think that Wayne was all that far from

167

understanding the truth, and it clearly helped to set him free. Charles Dickens personal journey also showed us how you can transmute pain to help yourself and others evolve. How we handle life's turbulence and injustices defines who we become. Processing pain can help us evolve or destroy us, underpinned by unconditional love or anger.

Maybe the human ideal of justice is not what God ever intended for his children; he knew it wouldn't help us to grow in character attitude and responsibility, or allow our souls to evolve. Let's hope that the muddled threads and knots of our lives help to create a masterpiece when finally seen from the other side, beyond the cradle and the grave. And if it does, I think it will be a masterpiece that expands beyond the human ego and self, genuinely becoming one with everything, including our Father in Heaven.

THE STARFISH STORY

It could be said that adults often think they know best. I think that the starfish story (a parable of sorts) explains this point far better than I can:

The story tells of a man walking along a beach after a terrible storm which has washed up thousands of starfish. A young girl was throwing starfish back into the water when the man questions the child's actions. The child points out that the sun is going down and that if she doesn't help them back into the ocean they will die. The adult rebuffs her, pointing out there are miles of beach and thousands of starfish; she can't possibly save them all, or make a significant difference. The child bends down, picks up a starfish, throws it back into the ocean and politely replies, "It made a difference to that one."

The moral of the story is we are often led to believe we can't make a difference by someone who thinks they know better or tells us we are wasting our time, but no good deed is ever wasted. No change is too small. I've learned in my time with Samaritans that even a smile or taking the time to listen to someone in distress can genuinely save a life. Looking back on my life, I've allowed the opinion of others to seriously derail my work, believing I couldn't make a difference. It took Wayne Dyer to help me understand that the good opinion of others is their business and not mine. That's not to say we shouldn't listen to others or seek wise counsel, but when all is said and done, we have to follow our own instincts and do what we think is right. In my experience, if this is done

169

with careful reflection, not to mention a sincere and open heart, it rarely goes awry.

At times while writing I've found myself wondering that, if the concept of justice is man-made, and ultimately impossible to achieve, what is the point of this book? One could almost say it even went wrong for God, and we see this time and time again in the Bible. Man became separated from him, a fallen angel rebelled, Adam was misled by Eve in the garden of Eden, the list goes on – but God didn't give up on his children. He tried to find a way to reconnect, and I don't know if those biblical stories are true or simply parables to help teach us how to find our way home. Does that matter? At the end of the day, it's what we take from those stories that makes the difference.

In life things will go wrong. That is guaranteed. I have never met a human who hasn't made a mistake or lost their way for a moment in time. Some greater than others, but everyone can find a way to influence change, one step at a time, starting with a single starfish. There might never be ultimate justice on Earth, but for a moment in time, one small heartfelt action can make a difference here on Earth as it is in Heaven.

We don't always see the end result of our actions, be them good or bad, but every cause has effect, and that effect ripples in ways we often don't imagine. I cannot tell you the number of times I was told I was wasting my time when stepping in to help a young person who was going off the rails in prison. I often used the starfish story to underpin why I felt it was worth investing in helping one young person find their way out of the storm. Life is not easy and I don't care who you are, Lord, Lady, CEO, Prince, policeman, or pauper; your actions can leave someone stranded on the beach fighting for their life, or they can help them to find their way home.

Nobody can help everyone or change the world completely. Just ask Jesus and God, they've been trying for over two thousand years; human beings have a knack for getting it wrong and falling short of the mark, but isn't that the substance of original sin, falling short of the mark? That said, we can all keep falling short, or we can recognise this fallacy, go beyond ourselves and change someone's world for the better, if we care enough to try.

Sometimes adults become more jaded as time goes by. One of the privileges of working around young adults and graduates is seeing that they still believe anything is possible. The problem is that the baggage, arrogance, ego and pain we collect as we age often weighs the soul, hampering our journey and limiting our actions and belief systems. So, whilst it's true that wisdom is earned with age, it's also important to never lose the child within or dampen someone's spirit in aid of efficacy. There is a marked difference between teaching someone *what* to think and teaching someone *how* to think; any great leader, parent or teacher knows this only too well. I also think it's something our Father in Heaven and Jesus understood, which is why he tried to teach us through parables. Each story has the power to lead someone to their own conclusion, in a way that makes sense to them individually.

I've often questioned why God sometimes seems to leave us hanging in the midst of so much chaos and confusion. To me, life often feels like a soap opera, or a giant cosmic game of *Cluedo* meets *Battleship* and *Monopoly*. I personally struggle to believe that our existence is the result of a random biological accident; this detracts from the majesty and intricate design at work in our universe. I like to think that we are either puppets in a mischievous creator's game, or cherished children with free will. You cannot have both, and I chose to believe we are the latter – it seems nicer, after all, to be considered cherished spiritual beings blessed with free will.

Maybe the answer to the chaos of creation is not unlike the story of the starfish – human arrogance stops us from helping our fellow neighbours and prevents us from nurturing creation in all its wonderous forms. Jesus pointed out that we should help the less fortunate and love one another, including our enemies, with unconditional love. When life's metaphorical storms leave us stranded on a beach, we all need someone to help pick us up and find our way back home. It's baffling to think that humanity already has the tools to help fix the world and support each other, we just don't seem to be able to use them. More often than not. we are like the adult on the beach who admonishes the child for even trying.

ARE YOU A TRAITOR OR A FAITHFUL?

For full disclosure, this chapter is a *late edition* to the publication. I've mentioned Wayne Dyer repeatedly throughout this book, but that is because it is so rare to find someone who inspires you to pick up your pen in favour of your sword, and when they do you never forget it. Wayne and I both believe in synchronicity when a situation occurs, and the stars align. Call it a miraculous event or not, we both know synchronistic events occur. Therefore, an unfolding of synchronicity encouraged me to add this chapter prior to publication.

I had been considering adding something on prayer, traitors and faithful's when the esteemed author Jeffery Archer gave me his most recent book called *Traitors Gate*. You see this book means more to me than mere words can say. There is another story behind each chapter, but much of that resides in faithful prayer between me and my maker.

That said, my intension to write a book was always known to two men more than most, both great authors in their own right. Oddly both Lords, if not the one residing in heaven, and both these slightly more human and political Lords certainly became the book ends to stabilise this book. Jeffery Archer and Dr Rowan Williams both ignited my passion to write and understood the background trauma, pain and injustice that was leveraged to sculpt every word in this book. They were both faithful to my journey and I wouldn't – actually, couldn't – have published this book before they had both read it first. They couldn't have been more delighted and encouraging in my journey.

I was deeply moved when Jeffery Archer stood in his own home holding an advanced proof of this book and went on to hand me a copy of his most recent book *Traitors Gate* saying, 'Bravo Chris, you did it, I am so proud of you.' But as I held his signed copy of *Traitors Gate*, which focused on crime, police, justice, traitors and faithfuls, I knew the universe or God was telling me to put one final chapter down in print. So, this is a bonus for you and routed in considered prayer. Because whilst I haven't mentioned prayer much in this book, I can assure you not a day goes by without me using the power of prayer.

Over the years I've come to realise not all prayers are answered on our (human) timeline, but I do think in the wider tapestry of life they are answered, even if we don't like the answer or the time it takes. There is a force behind prayer, and I encourage you to keep a prayer diary. It might take years, but like footprints in the sand and a glance in the rear-view mirror, given time you will see that prayers can be asked and answered.

If you live in the UK, or indeed even abroad now, then I am sure by now you have heard of the BBC show *The Traitors*. The show once again highlights humanity's love of intrigue, deception, murder and mayhem. The premise of the programme is you have Faithfuls and Traitors trying to reach the final of a murder mystery game in order to win a grand sum at the end of the show.

The programme has been clever in showing the art of deception and the way in which it only takes a single human being to manipulate an entire situation, often casting doubt into the wider group. However, *The Traitors* also has the ability to show the paradox of a Traitor building friendships with the people they are deceiving.

In the most recent UK series of *The Traitors,* one participant lost after letting her heart rule her head. The friendship she had built, and to some extent unconditional love, got in the way of her winning the grand prize. In post-show interviews this friendship appeared to have been restored, but one wonders if the relationship and her ability to trust will ever be the same again. Perhaps it will be; I believe that unconditional love can conquer all.

Jesus famously had to navigate the most well-known traitor of all time, Judas, who betrayed him for thirty pieces of silver.

Faith, be it Christianity or not, highlights all too well the irony of being faithful and being a traitor. A person's faith is so subjective and almost elusive by design, much like Our Father in Heaven can be at times. Jesus seemed to know he was going to be betrayed, and some of his last words on the cross were to his Father saying, 'Forgive them, for they know not what they have done'.

People of faith and none come in all shapes and sizes; not everyone starts out or ends up with the same level of faith they had during earlier periods of their lives. Some lose a faith in God and some find or strengthen their faith. I myself had two very different grandmothers. One was a card-carrying member of the Women's Institute. She was a talented cookery teacher and flower decorator who reminded me of the famous baker, Mary Berry. My other grandmother had no interest in cookery and would have adored the development of food delivery apps and the most up to date iPhone. She would happily go for a drink in the pub or have a curry, and she ran her own business well into her eighties. This grandmother often reminded me of a hybrid of the actress Joan Collins and late author Barbra Cartland, and she looked larger than life in pink. Certainly, a woman born before her time.

One gran grew old with grace, the other frankly never grew old at all, and at ninety was still acting as if she was nineteen – albeit in mind and spirit. I adored them both for and despite of their differences. During my childhood both ladies would meet and neither really understood each other's stance in life, but both came together out of a mutual love and respect for their family. The funny thing was that before the end of their lives, I would say that both of them had a profound faith which gave them comfort and joy. A faith that passed all understanding. It certainly gave them both peace. People of faith rarely approach it from the same trajectory – or even at the same times – and one person's faith and prayer life might differ from another. This is okay!

Last week, when I found myself sitting in the reception of Jeffery Archer's building in central London reading the paper, I was mindful that many people in the world would be wise to re-read the parable of the prodigal son in the bible, or even Jeffery Archer's book *Kane and Abel*. Life is too short for family disputes, misunderstandings and resentment. The prodigal son teaches us three things: repentance, forgiveness and redemption.

We and the media are so great at casting people as heroes and villains (or now, as traitors and faithfuls) and at times I think we all run the risk of straying between the faithful and traitor albeit in thought, word or deed. But we judge another man or woman's faith at our peril.

The real character or faith of any man, woman or child can only ever be understood by Our Father in Heaven. Without omnipotence, we can never come close enough to having absolute context on another human being. That's why I included my grandmothers' stories. They were both faithful, but had very different approaches to life and their faith in God – as we all do.

I remember touching on the issue of traitors more than once with a priest I respected more than most. William had a diverse journey working in one of the world's most notorious prisons and then going on to be a Chaplain for the late Queen Elizabeth before she passed. That man had a profound impact on my faith, and I respect him to this very day. I remember debating my concerns with him that people often use faith and religion as a mask for who they are. Anyone who has been or worked in a prison will know this, and it's a point currently being debated around asylum seekers and beyond. I will never forget William, the amazing priest that he was, pointing out that the reason why somebody approaches a bible or altar is their own business and should never detract from one's personal relationship with God; it should not stop them or another person from going to church.

That said, when debating faith and the most marginalised, we have to understand that exploitation can occur on both sides. The most broken and marginalised are ripe for the picking of preachers and people who claim everything can be fixed through faith and God, or via attending a faith-based course or too. Useful yes, but not always the ultimate answer to life's greatest questions.

In my experience, having a profound faith can bring peace in the eye of the storm, but it rarely, if ever, stops those storms, and it certainly never stops people from betraying you, whether their faith is real or not. This is something I think Charles Dickens understood better than most when he wrote in *Oliver Twist* that 'Dignity, and even holiness too, sometimes, are more questions of coat and waistcoat than some people imagine'.

I've mentioned before my resistance to organised religion, but I still find peace in attending church or taking communion. I don't believe everyone in a church or on the street has a genuine faith, but that's not my business. Any human being's relationship with God is between them and their Father in Heaven. Testimony is important, but as any person with lived experience knows, a good story or testimony will be exploited by people to further their own cause or agenda.

I suppose that the only comfort I have is knowing that I have seen people who play the system first hand, but I have also known that the word of God does often reach them, in some small way. Being a Faithful or a Traitor is subjective, partly because people are so multifaceted. The issue is feelings and emotions (be them love, confusion, anger or hate) so often define us, but things aren't always black and white. As the shield on the cover of this book shows all too clearly, there are also shades of grey in us all. Another quote of Dickens which highlights this point is, 'No one is useless in this world who lightens the burdens of another'.

Without doubt, I believe that people who claim to have faith, people who often go to church, or those who do not, hold a relationship with their creator in Heaven, whether they have faith in that or not. It's also important to understand that God isn't just in a church or in Heaven; he's in every stream, mountain, atom, molecule or flower, and he is inside us. Be you faithful or traitor, the closer we get to him, the more the traitor inside will ebb, and the prize of getting closer to Our Father in Heaven is way beyond any pot of gold. The prize is being or becoming faithful and true.

After all, as I once said to my former Member of Parliament after he fought my corner for compensation when my multi award-winning work was completely derailed, 'one day the truth will set me free!' Looking back, I had no idea how relevant, profound and ironic those heartfelt words would turn out to be. Thank God, the pen is mightier than the sword, and for the faithfuls we meet along the way. Especially when we sometimes encounter a traitor in our midst.

CHILDREN ARE THE FUTURE

As I've stated continually throughout this book, children are unquestionably our future, and the greatest love in existence has to be unconditional love. Not just for the world and all of humanity, but for ourselves. I don't mean an egoistic love, but a connected understanding and respect for who we are in mind, body and spirit; we are part of one family and one world, whether we like it or not. We have to teach our children to first believe in themselves and then love who they truly are, or else they will never come close to loving the world around them – at least certainly not in any meaningful way.

'The Greatest Love of All', often sung by Whitney Houston, is a clear reminder that words are important but not enough. God alone knows how many times Whitney sang the lyrics. Sadly, her life and profound talent didn't always mirror the words she sang, as her astonishing life showed all too profoundly. Her pain and battles were like so many of ours – rooted in emotional storms, chaos, pain and addictions that swirl us off course, starfish on the sand. It wasn't until a few years ago that I felt the energy and power an artist like Whitney or George Michael would have faced time and again – that sense of putting their heads above the parapet and stepping out on stage, waiting to be applauded and judged by their fellow man – on a scale few mere mortals will ever understand. Overpowering, all-consuming and unreal. Truly like chasing the dragon.

There's a hint of this sensation when you stand or sit in the rafters of a stadium – often called the gods, a term first coined in theatre. I first noticed it myself when I was in Wembley Stadium listening to Fleetwood Mac sing 'Don't Stop'. I had just stepped into the foyer to buy a drink for some friends and as I returned into the stadium proper and looked down, the force of humanity and the energy of more than 50,000 people hit me like a brick. Everyone was on a high, but it was an unrealistic high which our world seems to embrace above all else. We go chasing daily for highs of various kinds to either make us feel alive or blunt the pain, storms and realities of life. The kind of energy which artists like Whitney and many other celebrities face can be all encompassing. All too often, they become nothing more than a commodity at the hands of others, or a media soundbite to be exploited.

Whitney Houston was right when she sang about children holding the key to our future. The pen is mightier than the sword, but what's behind the words is often the greatest lesson we can teach our kids. When they grow up, we desperately need for them to have a discernment for truth and an unconditional love in their hearts, or frankly humanity doesn't stand a chance.

When I looked down on humanity from the top of Wembley Stadium, the thousands in the crowd and their energy blended together, appearing to become one. As Mick Fleetwood, the co-founder of the band, lit by thousands of phone flashlights closed the show with 'Don't Stop', he also cautioned us all to be kind to one another and to never stop thinking about tomorrow.

I remember thinking this as I observed the people; everyone here has their own story, families, friends, children back home, or on the way. They are all brimming with infinite potential, joys, heartbreaks and sorrows to come, but from a distance, and for one moment in time, they all came together in peace, light and harmony. After all, isn't that the meaning of life and where we really find justice? It's certainly where we find our Father in Heaven, congregated, at one, with absolutely no separation.

ONE MOMENT IN TIME
The Epilogue

The first thing I wanted to say was thank you for taking the time to get to the end of the book and for joining me on the journey. I've written a few books before but never actually published them – partly because when I did write the drafts, I felt that I was still in the eye of a storm and trying to find my way out. I firmly believe that if a book (or anything for that matter) isn't written with love in your heart, it runs the risk of causing more harm than good.

Earlier I mentioned the song 'Mary Did You Know', which asks whether she knew her son Jesus had come to save us. Jesus is meant to be our creative force and Father in Heaven, returned in human form to deliver humanity to eternal life. I'm always mindful that Jesus said humans were made in God's image, and humanity is certainly a creative force. I hope throughout this book I have shown that any creative force can be used for good or bad, be it a word, parent, teacher, leader an atom – split or otherwise – or a gun to protect and destroy.

Humanity's latest global creation is AI, or artificial intelligence. It's so relevant at the time of writing this book, that the word AI has been included into the Oxford English dictionary as a word of the year, and my editor will be running these pages through an AI checker shortly after she receives them. Maybe it's time to understand that what gave the Bible so much power and influence was metaphor and parable. We are cautioned not to judge ourselves, but that Jesus will return to judge the living and the dead. We are told that he wanted to save us from original sin, which is essentially falling short of the mark. With AI, the possibilities are currently endless. Humanity is teetering on an unknown frontier, the likes of which have only been considered in sci-fi books and films up to this point. Isn't it thought-provoking that AI might one day help humanity to cure a blind man. Maybe it will help us to walk on water or create life from a virgin; it could even find ways to raise man from the dead and give us eternal life in some form or another. I actually do believe in Jesus and I don't mean to be irreverent by making these suggestions; I just want to propose a thought in metaphor and parable.

One day, AI might become humanity's saviour, but it might also become separated from us and become humanity's greatest original sin. We already fear this, a sensation wired into us called the uncanny valley. What would happen if AI were to put humanity on trial without context, considering all the evidence before it? Could we possibly be found innocent with the way we sometimes act? Would we pass the threshold of reasonable doubt without considered context? And then, could AI become our judge, jury and executioner – rather than our saviour? After all, parents judge children and children grow up judging parents, and humanity continually judges each other. It's a vicious cycle. What difference is there to be found in artificial intelligence created and programmed by man?

This book was aimed at highlighting that justice is almost impossible and frequently rooted in judgements made by all who nurture children and help them grow. But, as wonderful as humanity is, it also shows we consistently fall short. Our greatest frequent sin is that we are shocking custodians of the Earth and each other, a fact I pray might change given time. The problem is that human beings often think and act like God when they are not. We might be part of him and his creation, but the moment we think we are God, just because we can create something, we are falling into very dangerous territory. If we are ever judged by artificial intelligence, isn't it worth considering that, only through following the ten commandments laid down in stone thousands of years ago, we might be found free of sin and not condemned for falling short of the mark? Once again, I'm not trying to be irreverent; I'm simply pointing out that anything created is judged by its creator – think of *Frankenstein* – and all too often the creation and, everything around it, frequently ends up judging the creator. It's certainly food for thought. Who hasn't considered or judged our creator or Father in Heaven, whether they believe in him or not?

This brings me back to the start; it all begins with the words. So, I reaffirm, be careful what you say, because children will hear you; be careful what you do as they will be watching closer than you might think – and most worrying, at times they may turn to you to discover who they are. Artificial, intelligent or not.

Many years ago, I sat talking to the author Jeffery Archer about writing my first book. Beyond the editing advice he gave me, he also reminded me that the most important thing when writing was to never cheat the reader. So, I guess that whilst the book you've just read isn't directly about me or my story, you might still be wondering who I am, and what my experience in prisons and justice actually is. Well, it's lived experience. I had a number of operations as a child, missed a lot of school and certainly had general anxiety disorder. I became an addict to prescription medication, at first to combat physical pain, but it quickly became used to cover emotional pain. Likewise, my father was a lovely man but an alcoholic. For a while my life became like a hybrid of the films *Catch Me If Can (based on the true story of Frank Abagnale)* and *The Firm (based on a John Grisham legal thriller)*, where I ran from the world and myself, causing unintentional chaos in my wake. Much like Charles Dickens showed in *Oliver Twist*, some of the people I ran towards and trusted, whilst in pain, were not good people, and their influence trapped me in a destructive web for more than a moment in time, and I didn't know who to turn to or how to break free. I certainly became lost before I was found, and blind before I could see.

That changed through grace, a profound faith and facing my demons head on, some self-made, but many made by my fellow man. As you can see, I have approached Lady Justice confessing that I am both guilty and innocent at times. I have plead guilty and plead not guilty in my life, and there were reasons and profound truths behind both statements of fact at different stages in my life. I can assure you, any time spent behind bars, depending on those honest statements of innocence and guilt, is a very different experience. One is a justice, and the other sears your soul. Just look at the impact on the sub-postmasters and mistresses caught up in the post office scandal. I've encountered justice from all sides and also felt what it's like to have people crucify you for falsities, denying that they know you when faced with trial, as you plead for truth and justice to prevail. They leave you to a fate of profound injustice as they turn their backs on you.

I wish to God I could turn back time on some things, but as much as we try, we can't. And as Elton John put it so succinctly, sorry is often the hardest word, but at times I have been sorry, and at times I've been hurt by others too. God only knows whether they are sorry, but that fact no longer matters.

I'm certainly no Jeffery Archer, Charles Dickens or Rudyard Kipling, just a mere fledgling writer, but like Jeffery Archer I have been in prison. Oddly enough, I have also worked around the justice system and rehabilitation projects too. I've mentored law students and taken them around prisons. I've been supported by prison officers, governors and probation officers at various times in my life and been humbled by their work – and I've worked alongside a few in prisons and beyond. I've had business partners who were former police officers and prison governors and been mentored by global business leaders. I call some people who work on the front line my closest friends – and trust me, many are hidden heroes, but not all. I've admired police and been horrified by them, met great lawyers and shocking ones, the same with judges and offenders in prison and beyond – recognising that behind the labels, they are only human after all. That said, there are also many police, judges, probation staff, and lawyers who I admire and am honoured to call my friends. As Wayne Dyer would have put it, they've all been my teachers, but none more than the young adults I've worked with along the way.

Just before the pandemic hit, I unexpectedly found myself in prison again and robustly tried to appeal my conviction. Covid, costs and lockdown made that process far harder than I can ever explain – as did my past and access to effective legal counsel. In the end, I realised I couldn't get back the time lost, and for many reasons I want to forget the past and move on, and after this book I doubt I will ever talk about prison, law or justice again. Writing it is a form of closure – making sure the journey and my historic award-winning work wasn't an entire waste.

And it wasn't a waste, due to one thing that happened in lockdown. Because of my past work, a governor asked me to move on to and stay on the young adult wing to help mentor the men – as not long before my arrival, one young man had chosen to take his own life. The prison staff and management knew of my work before prison and my background with the Samaritans, mental health advocacy and suicide prevention, and asked that I not waste it – despite being in the eye of my own storm. None of us expected the pandemic to hit weeks later, and that experience forced me towards a level of insight and maturity that I didn't think possible, and a faith that kept me safe in the eye of the storm. At times the experience was like being in a war zone.

Only recently, whilst I was taking my mother to the hospital for an MRI scan, I bumped into a former prison officer who was at the time responsible for taking care of me and my peers, and we both noted that we had been diagnosed with PTSD following the experience, albeit we approached it from very different perspectives. It wasn't until that day, as we met on the top of the hospital stairs and caught up, I learned that he was the one who found the young man after he'd taken his own life just before I arrived on the wing. Never underestimate the things people working on the front line are faced with day in day out. The things people do to themselves and each other – it's why so many are hidden heroes. That astonishing man was so traumatised by the experience of the job, he left the service and now works as a maintenance man in a hospital and as an author himself. He never stopped caring and I saw first-hand the difference his humanity made to many broken young men, simply because he cared and treated all the men in his care with humility, respect, and compassion. He certainly helped me at some of the lowest points in the pandemic – and many of my friends.

I have great respect for people working on the front line, and for the recent decision of the Ministry of Justice in the UK to highlight the benefits and stark realities in recent films made to support their recruitment process. Becoming a hidden hero on the front line isn't a walk in the park, but when done for the right reasons, it's one of the greatest jobs anyone could ever undertake, because it genuinely changes lives.

Despite the legacy of my own PTSD, the experience taught me what it means to feel like a father figure to a number of broken young souls. They taught me more about humanity than any AI programme, Bible, archbishop or sermon ever could. The good, the bad and the ugly sides of humanity. I often see some of the young men in the street walking to work, and occasionally meet a former member of staff. I'm always mindful that there is a smile, shaking of hands, clap on the back, hug or fist bump of respect from them. Whether being behind bars as a prisoner or as a member of staff or volunteer, walking on the front line is an experience only few human beings will ever have.

So, I know why Jesus mentioned the point albeit metaphorically, 'Did you visit me when I was in prison?' – because few people ever really do. Christianity often hits the morality of justice head on – or uses it in metaphor and parable to explain humanity and sin, original or otherwise.

The reason I was once used to go on a leadership programme was to be the voice of the most marginalised for major employers and global brands – and I use the word 'used' with considered reflection, because I was used by nearly everyone involved, possibly before I was ready. I'm a maverick, I'm a Christian, I've been broken, I've judged others and been judged, I've been rich, and I've been poor, I've been homeless and lived in wonderful homes. I've been guilty and I've been innocent, I've won multiple awards for my work and had success and I've made my own share of mistakes. I've been a mentor and I've been mentored; I've tried to take my own life and I've been a Samaritan working to prevent suicide, I've been a bookseller and become a published author, I've been a leadership fellow at St George's House Windsor Castle and helped to nurture future leaders. I've helped and saved people often from themselves, and I've found some redemption along the way. But I have never really understood man's ability to create chaos, frequently in the name of truth, justice and liberty for all, and I'm not sure I ever will. I guess that's why I believe in good and evil – being human has to be a spiritual battle; nothing else makes much sense.

Human beings are complex, and whilst I've never had kids of my own, for one moment in time when the world came to a standstill, I tried to be a father figure to countless young men – some of the hardest to reach on the planet, and the evidence when I meet them years later proves I did a fairly good job. Some wrote me thank you letters that touched my very soul, and more than one even said they wished I was their father. Their words mean vastly more than any awards I've ever won, or the brief time I spent as a leadership fellow at St George's House Windsor Castle ironically trying to tackle mental health, social justice and prison reform.

I don't want to write about my own story as it's too multifaceted, painful and confusing; and besides that, even an editor from Harper Collins said it was far too complex for just one book, and that was years before the story became really interesting. That said, the wisdom behind and within my personal journey might help one person – or save a life – and as somebody who was taken to the brink of suicide more than once knows, life is for living and we need to learn to live before we die.

To close, I would use three words that sum up justice to me accountability, fairness and peace. Man's justice is often focused on judgement, punishment and occasionally revenge. God's justice is centred on restoration, grace and unconditional love. Humanity is certainly changing around how it perceives crime, punishment and justice, placing rehabilitation at the heart of the process. But in a world that judges and condemns everything day in day out, often in the name of entertainment and social media, and often wildly without context, let alone any flavour of reality, it's not changing quickly enough to save itself from itself. Remember an eye for an eye would leave the whole world blind, and taking all of the earth's resources without replenishing them will leave a barren and broken planet. I don't have all the answers, but eternal truths are signposts we so often ignore at our peril, and nearly 2000 years ago I believe someone walked the earth trying to act as an intervention between our creator and ourselves. My guess is that, with the way we are going, it's time for the next intervention, because without it, who will be left holding the baby?

As I look around the world today, I struggle to find even three wise men or woman watching over us in any meaningful way. Leadership should be about leadership, not lobbying and ego. Every baby should be born with a star to guide them and a safe place to lay their head. That certainly isn't the case in a world where 1% control so much more than they should, and flawed leaders drop bombs like confetti at a wedding. Humanity needs to wake up and smell the roses before we become extinct. We have turned the human race into a chaotic game of chance, judgement, want, manipulation, commercialism and ego. Parents do an incredible job, but how can they alone make sure that children have a future, when they are so often not in control of the game?

I often ask people if they could pick one song what would it be, partly because I found it helps to reveal what's in someone's heart and soul, or at least helps to underline what's important to them. For a while my song was 'If I Could Turn Back Time', but now I have two choices; 'Healer of My Heart' and 'One Moment in Time'. One is a prayer that shows you can't go at it alone, and in my case my heart and soul certainly needed some help – without it I wouldn't have survived or ever written this book. The other one is an emotional outcry that at some point in time I want to achieve all I can be, and I don't want any of that to be artificial. Just firmly rooted in some intelligence, compassion and humanity I've found along the way, recognising like everyone I am still a work in progress. To that end, I will continue to write a collection of books under *Published with Love* and learn to listen to people who know more than me, many do – and hopefully not die with my music still in me.

Until we meet again, please remember that your voice and the pen in your hand are mightier than the sword, so use them wisely; let's try to find at least three wise men or women to help bring peace on earth. Leaders who lead without ego or personal agenda. People who unconditionally love their fellow human beings. Because until that day, we will never really come close to finding justice, let alone peace on Earth and goodwill to all men, women and children.

One man or woman can tip the balance of justice with one small thing, so finding it is often almost impossible. This doesn't mean that the pursuit of justice isn't worth the effort, when all is said and done.

SPECIAL NOTE

*If you are struggling with mental health issues and thoughts of suicide or need to talk to somebody in confidence, please reach out to a friend, a medical professional or support system like MIND, The Big White Wall or the Samaritans in the UK by Calling **116123** for free or email jo@samaritans.org*

*In the US, you can reach out to the AFSP (American Foundation for Suicide Prevention), call **988** Suicide and Crisis Lifeline 24/7, or text **TALK** to **741741** - Information at www.suicidepreventionlifeline.org*

Otherwise, please find a local suicide prevention organisation in your country. Ask a Nurse, Doctor or friend and find someone who's good at listening. Talking helps and remember; no storm lasts forever.

ACKNOWLEDGMENTS

If it takes a village to raise a child, it takes the world to raise a man, woman or author for better or worse. In my case there have been so many people who have made an impact on my work and ability to write, including the good, the bad and the ugly. All have been some of my greatest teachers. That said, a few have played a significant part behind the scenes and helped me to become who I am today. Most notably Our Father in Heaven. This book is for humanity and for the people I have met along the way. Whether my life touched you for better or worse, I sincerely hope the pen has proven mightier than the sword - going on to give context to the journey that led to becoming a man and vastly better author and human-being. I guess behind the complex threads and knots, this book is just a mere tapestry which gives light and understanding to all the friendships, relationships and various interactions on the journey of life.

My greatest thanks have to go to my family, those now residing in heaven and those still on earth, especially my mother who helped give me life, stood by my side in the eye of some of life's greatest storms, and steadied my hand as I picked up my pen. I love you with all my heart and soul, and admire your resilience of spirit and kindness.

My astonishing illustrator Marianne Lang; working with you on this book has been an utter joy. Not to mention my formidable and talented book editor, Rowan Maddock. I only made it to the point of publishing because of your collective talents and encouragement. I consider you to be colleagues, collaborators and friends, and can't wait to start working with you both on the next book. This is our book, not mine. Wayne Dyer was right – when you're ready, the right people come into your life – especially a very talented illustrator and editor.

To my wonderful former colleagues at Waterstones, you helped me become an amazing bookseller and gave me a safe haven in the eye of the odd storm. Without you all, I wouldn't have wanted to publish this book, nor been able to!

Next, I have to thank my dear friend (and brother) Justin, Tracy and his amazing family. Justin, you are my hero. You have been the wind beneath my wings for more years than I care to mention, and the fuel for all my work, including this book. Not to mention every title, draft and edit that came before! Justin, you are the best listener I have ever met, and an amazing friend, father and human being. Not to mention Jason, Guy, Frankie (AKA *A Cat Bob*) and Lee (AKA *Scrubby*) – my original peers. Without you all being by my side for more decades than I care to remember, I wouldn't have wanted to nor been able to write this book. Jason, you taught me first-hand the power of unconditional love and that anyone can be a father figure or role model to somebody who needs guidance, and that not all families come with the same DNA. Jason, you will always be like a son to me. You are certainly the cornerstone of all my work and why I had to write this book – for you, Scrubby and our peers.

Which brings me to Alvin and the other Chipmunks I met along the way (my peers) you know who you are, this book is really for you – a total fist-bump of respect! As Wayne Dyer would say, you became my greatest teachers!

Jane Rose, my former business partner. My little caped crusader, your career path is diverse, profound and admirable. I admire your strength of character and determination to help your friends, family and other people through their own storms. Not to mention your critical eye over the final edits of this book! Our friendship, historic multi-award-winning work - *LEARN2LISTEN* (and this book) proves nothing is ever wasted.

I cannot move forward without thanking the lady who taught me and my peers to listen. A truly good *Samaritan*! My friend the late great Kathy Baker MBE and her amazing sister Jan and her husband Glyn. You have stood by me at every stroke of the pen, and your friendship and prayers have certainly helped this book to be born.

Profound thanks to an amazing lady and friend whose work always has a long queue outside her office door. Christine Baker, you inspire so many people who find themselves looking over a cliff edge or at a crossroads. I couldn't have achieved anything like I have without you – including this book or becoming all things *Book-ish*.

I also have to thank my amazing former colleagues and family at *Book-ish Cafe* in Crickhowell. Emma and Drew, including all the customers. Most notably Ioan (if legend is to be believed Ioan means a gift from God, which explains a lot) and Sue who became a lifelong friend and encouraged me to write a book only a few short months ago. I listened and put pen to paper.

To my friends and family in Christ. Dr Rowan Williams, your humility, friendship, considered prayers and faith certainly inspired me to write. What a journey from Canterbury to Cardiff. Rowan, the first day we met, we talked about my new ability to write being a gift from God. I hope this book honours that reflection. Dr Barry Morgan (*former Archbishop of Wales*) your consideration, prayers and support strengthened my faith and belief in humanity and played a part in the context of this book. Joy and Tim Watson, your support of the Car Strategy and my wider work became a cornerstone to this book. My dearest go-to friends and prayer partners Oris Ikomi and Norma. Your faith, humility and unconditional love gives me hope in humanity, and faith in God.

One of my former Wavelength Connect and St George's House Society of Leadership peers – Tess, who stood by me and inspired much of my work. Tess, you taught me how to rise from the ashes of adversity, the power of sharing and preventing waste – not to mention that anything is possible. Even writing a book or two! The first titles and drafts certainly fed into this book proving that all our work can be shared, recycled and not wasted. You truly have the wingspan of an eagle when in flight. Not to mention your amazing stepdaughter, Yas, who taught me the power of nurturing law students, and that there is hope for ethical lawyers to be born beyond university and the bar.

Jeffery Archer, who made me smile, encouraged me to write, and taught me the power of editing until the end of time. Lord Archer, I got there in the end!

Thank you to James Reed CBE for giving me some amazing books, including your own publications *Why You* and *Put Your Mindset to Work*. Not to mention for helping me to put my own mindset to work and go on to inspire me to publish my own collection of books. Once I started to write this, I realised *I love Mondays*.

Possibly the greatest Governor and gentleman I met along the journey, Ash – you're definitely a hidden hero, with a profound faith and humanity - a real class act. We met nearly a decade ago when I was working on my first book. That draft was never published but certainly laid a cornerstone for this book's narrative and everything to come.

To Ray and Vi, for inspiring me that restorative justice is the key to rehabilitation and placing victims first is always paramount. Not to mention that unconditional love can bring healing. Your beliefs are a cornerstone to the integrity of this book.

Followed by the amazing: Governors Ceri, Glen, Elfed, Mark, Janet and front-line staff; Shari, Loui, Tom, Callum, Alison, Darren, Karen, Mark, Elvis, Mel, Amanda, Steve, Frank, Olivia, Lucy, Pat, Emma, Hana, Sonia and Claire. Not to mention the best front-line officer I ever met, Ollie – you are my hidden hero and a governor in the making! The astonishing and compassionate Sally, who helped me to teach my peers about the power of reading and opening a book. Every turn of the page made a difference – make sure they read this one!

Not forgetting my dear friends and life's fellow storm slayers: Jordan, James, Darren, Ned, Jackie, Todd, Raphael, Steve, Val, Tina, Martin, Christel, Rosie, Gaynor, Rob, Billy, Jacky, Renda, Carol, Val, Colin, Derek, Paul, Mark, Ed, Adam, Andrew (And), Marcello, Stephen, Scottish Neil, Penelope, Cagney, Lisel, Issac, Sheena, Paul (Ted), Ruth, Sarah, Pete, Natalie, Kevin, Vicky, Lacey, Eleri, Stephen, Rory and David.   Your friendship, encouragement and support played a foundational part to my journey - not to mention each stroke of the pen.

Marc, who watched from afar and encouraged me to write while nodding in sympathy during the final edits and gave some profound insights into the cover. Not to mention, inspired the section that touched on Madonna for the very first time.

Guinevere and Ringo, for being stars and sitting alongside me, or under the desk purring as I worked on each and every bloody draft. Your unconditional love reminds me of why animals are a gift from

God and inspiration. I've even forgiven Guinevere (HRH) for walking over the keyboard and deleting a page or two.

Michael and Eve, who gave me a safe haven and encouraged me to pick up my pen and write. Not to mention thank you for teaching me about the Windrush generation; you are both a credit to its legacy.

My work/business coaches, Paul and Marc, your belief in the book and future publications really helped give me the courage to put pen to paper, carefully reflect and publish.

My dear friend Fergus, who was the first person I talked to about this book, its wider concept and why I wanted to write it. Your humour, intelligence and ability to say it as it is encouraged me to go for it. Thank you for all your support!

The wonderful Liam in the Library – a true gent and inspiration. If it wasn't for your kindness and consideration, I wouldn't have made it through the most recent storm, let alone written this book.

My friends and family at the Samaritans and all the Listeners. Not to mention my fellow Listener the late great author journalist Erwin James. The integrity of your work inspired me and a generation and left a profound legacy around prison reform that I have no doubt will live on. I hope this book honours that legacy.

Chris Hill for supporting so much of my journey, encouraging me to become a bookseller and author. Hey, Chris its finally happened, and partly thanks to you!

Gethin Jones, my friend peer and fellow author. Our journey has been broad and diverse, often routed in a shared understanding of the profound potential in the care system, and behind bars in the revolving doors of the prison systems around the world. We both lost friends to suicide and addiction – it's why working on the frontline matters, especially your work! I hope you know this book honour our journey and mutual love of all things Charles Dickens! What power resides in conquering a dark night of the soul.

Reverend Edward Cearns (Ed) Your friendship, faith and journey inspired me for decades. I will never forget your support in the early days, not to mention the guidance on earlier publications that never made it to print. Everything laid a cornerstone to creating this book. We both understand taking our time to get it right is worth the wait! Cambridge and the Church are lucky to have you.

Reverends Jonathan Aitken and Paul Cowley MBE for igniting my passion in prison ministry, social justice – and your astonishing work to help our peers find faith and get into sustainable employment. You always had time to listen and became the fuel to believe in life after labels. You both helped to ignite my passion to help my peers, something routed in every page of this book.

All my friends and former Leadership Fellows from St George's House at Windsor Castle, for helping me to understand the power of nurturing future leaders behind the historic Castle walls.

The Wavelength Connect Alumni, for being on the Same Wavelength most of the time, and for Liam, who taught me to challenge everything – including religion, embrace leadership and being a Maverick, not to mention the power of straight talking. David, for always being at the end of a phone and acting as wise counsel, not to mention for locating Paddington 2 – a gift beyond all gifts.

My Friends, peers and wise counsel, Whitney and Denise, you both inspired me and cared when care was needed most. Humbled to know you both and call to you friends. You are part of the suspension in the pages of this book.

My great friend Neil, your experience in law enforcement and safeguarding across a whole spectrum of the criminal justice system inspired much of my work. Wow. What a journey we've had over the last decade, but we got there in the end, and proved safeguarding in the church and on the front line really matters. Together, we made a difference.

My adopted family at the Freedom Centre in Sheerness. You, more than most, taught me the power of unconditional love. You are giants in spirit and grace. Not to mention comedians who always look on the bright side of life, even when there is a hole in your bucket. This book is for you and Dennis.

To the adopted sister (and her family) who bought me my first balloon, it turned out to be an Airwalker that helped me walk on air, albeit for a moment in time. Even when the balloons either lost their helium or floated towards the heavens, the love lasted forever.

To Emma for taking the time to listen and counsel me on everything in the background, including bypassing the pain barrier. Your support helped me to create, publish and promote the book. Helping to smooth out the emotional journey!

Christopher Shreeve – you are the Superman to my Clarke Kent. Together we have navigated the Kryptonite which life sometimes placed in our path.

Last, but certainly not least; Dr Wayne Dyer and your family. Without you, I wouldn't still be alive or able to see clearly now the rain has gone. I would never have considered writing this book without being fortunate enough to meet you – The Father of Motivation and a fellow Scurvy Elephant (*disturbing element*) – before you passed. I think your statement, 'Writing isn't something I do, writing is something that I am. I am writing - it's just an expression of me' says it all. I hope to follow in your footsteps and that profound sentiment, albeit in some small way.

Wayne, this book is metaphorically what was inside me when I squeezed the orange. Thanks to you, I haven't died with my music still in me. The storm didn't last forever!

THE END

Illustrations by Marianne Lang

Printed in Great Britain
by Amazon

38374144R00116